To
Cecelia
may God bless
and keep you as
you live a focused
life as you live the
Lord's Prayer!

F.O.C.U.S.

LIVING THE
LORD'S PRAYER

Jeremiah 29:11

F.O.C.U.S.

LIVING THE LORD'S PRAYER

TYRONE D. GORDON

Abingdon Press
Nashville

Library of Congress Cataloging-in-Publication Data

Gordon, Tyrone.
    F.O.C.U.S. : living the Lord's prayer / Tyrone D. Gordon.
       p. cm.
    Includes bibliographical references and index.
    ISBN 978-0687-64474-2 (binding: pbk., adhesive perfect : alk. paper)
    1. Lord's prayer.   I. Title.

BV230.G63 2008
226.9′606—dc22

2007045149

08 09 10 11 12 13 14 15 16 17—10 9 8 7 6 5 4 3 2 1
MANUFACTURED IN THE UNITED STATES OF AMERICA

CONTENTS

ACKNOWLEDGMENTS

Prayer has been a part of my life as long as I can remember. My understanding of it has grown with age, experience, and life. I must take the time to thank those persons and congregations who poured so much into my life and ministry, who by their touch taught me how to pray.

I thank God for my beautiful and supportive family, my wife, Marsha, who is always there through thick and thin; she has helped shoulder many burdens and is the cause of countless joys! Thank you for not only teaching me to pray but praying with and for me. My two princesses of daughters, Lauren and Allyson, you two are the joy of my life and I love you both; thank you for teaching me how to pray.

To my mother, Mrs. Jean Gordon (Mama), and my grandmother, Mrs. O. V. Smith (Nana), who instilled in me the value of prayer and its importance as the foundation upon which to build my life and ministry. Mama, thank you for teaching Cynthia, Keith, and me how to pray. And even when we did not want to learn it, you taught us that our power came when we were on our knees. Mama and Nana, I love you both for who you are and what you taught me about life, family, and the Lord!

To the church of my youth, the Mount Moriah Baptist Church in Los Angeles, California, who, along with our late pastor and his wife, the Reverend Earl A. Pleasant and Mrs. Olga M. Pleasant, instilled in me the principal elements of prayer, how it works, and how God uses us and a congregation when we pray; to those saints past and present of "the Mount," thank you! The memories of those all-night prayer meetings and vigils are firmly planted in the beloved memories of my soul. I miss you, Pastor and Mrs. Pleasant; you taught me how to pray.

Thanks to the beloved congregations I have served in my ministry, who helped shape my prayer life and worked with me to establish prayer as a priority in congregational life. In particular, thank you to the members of Saint Mark United Methodist Church in Wichita who helped me pray and covered me in prayer as we built a great ministry and witness known throughout this nation. To my present congregation, my beloved St. Luke "Community" United Methodist Church in Dallas, thank you for your support, prayers, and words of encouragement. As we continue to cover our prophetic witness in prayer, you are there! Thank you for teaching me how to pray.

To Dr. Zan Holmes, Jr., the one who built St. Luke "Community" United Methodist Church into the powerful witness for the kingdom it is. Thank you for believing in me and modeling the image of the spiritual and social dimensions of a prayerful life. Thanks, Doc, for all you have poured into my ministry and career; you taught me how to pray.

To the brothers who are my Prayer Partners, who pray for me daily, I thank you all for your counsel, support, gentle pushes, and prayers in completing this project! Thanks, Harry, Derek, Cottrell, Kevin, J. D., Dale, Rick, Art, Vince, Dante, Kelvin, Kenneth, Shump, Chris, Keith, Robert, and Jim. Thank you, brothers, for being my partners in prayer! Also, thanks, to my sisters and brothers in my Incubator Group, in particular Rudy Rasmus, Vance Ross, and Joe Daniels, who pushed me and prodded me to get this project done! I thank God for placing all of you in my life; truly you all are teaching me how to pray.

I would be remiss if I did not thank the readers who reviewed each chapter and sent back their comments and corrections. A shout-out and thanks go out to: my wife, Marsha Gordon, Angela Woodson, Arthur Ballard, Arthur Gregg, Dale Watson, Derek Jacobs, Harry Christian, Justin Coleman, Kelvin Walker, Marge Kimbrough (Mom #2), Shirley Isom-Newsome, and Thomas Spann, Jr. Your candor and honesty helped me greatly with this project. Thank you for teaching me how to pray.

Last but not least, I want to thank my staff at St. Luke "Community" and in particular my administrative assistant, Ms. Carolyn Howard, for guarding my time during this project and pushing and nudging me along. Ms. Carolyn, thank you for being a strong prayer warrior and for praying for me. Watching and working with you has taught me how to pray.

F.O.C.U.S.—LIVING A LIFE OF PRAYER

Lord, teach us to pray. —Luke 11:1

It all hit me one morning in the spring of 1992 in Wichita, Kansas. While serving the Saint Mark United Methodist Church, I had given all I had to give but I had drained myself in the process. That alone was part of the problem—I thought I needed to replenish myself. After five years in a fast-growing congregation and being touted as a "successful" pastor, I was running on spiritual fumes. On the outside, everything looked fine; but on the inside, I was sinking in a pit of despair, sinking fast! My tank was empty, and little did I know that morning, I was about to run completely out of spiritual gas. In spite of doing all the right things in moving that ministry forward and experiencing phenomenal growth in the process, I was doing all the wrong things to keep myself spiritually fed and nourished. I was trying to ride on the fumes of success, the fumes of church growth, the fumes of conference leadership, even the fumes of the applause of peers; but I soon discovered that those things won't keep you running for long. I was like a dehydrated marathon runner; I was about to crash and burn.

Sometimes life drives home lessons that we can never forget as well as things we should never forget. But more important, these hard times can help us grow into focused and committed disciples the Lord is calling for today. Some things will *drive us* to our knees, but being *driven to our knees* can be a good thing, because it is there that God will teach us to pray.

As I entered my office that Tuesday morning, I was com-pletely overwhelmed by a spirit of frustration, emptiness, and depression. As I sat down at my desk I literally broke down in uncontrollable tears. I cried like a baby! I had given so much and there was nothing more left to give. While basking in the glow of success, I felt like a failure. As I look back on it today, I must have been on the edge of a breakdown. My secretary at the time, Rita, heard me; and I still don't know what prompted her to do this, but instead of coming to me, she quickly called my wife, Marsha. Marsha in turn called my dear friend and brother in min-istry, the Reverend Henry "Hank" Wilkins, who at the time was serving a local church in Dallas. Within the hour, he jumped in a car and drove the six hours from Dallas to Wichita, Kansas, to get me! Thank God for friends and fam-ily who see you in a crisis and intervene before it is too late.

When Hank arrived, Marsha had a bag packed for me. Hank told me to get in the car, and then he took me to Dallas to reflect, retool, and refocus! I am so glad they and God stepped in right on time! That time away changed my life. I began to see the importance of pastors retooling and refilling themselves on a continual basis.

Prayer took on a new role in my life, my ministry, and in the church. I had always heard my mentor and predecessor, Dr. Zan Wesley Holmes, Jr., tell us in seminary that we preachers need to be in the Word to hear a word from the Lord *for ourselves* and not just to preach a word *to others*!

Preachers need to hear God speak through the Bible and we should not just open it to find a sermon.

YOU CAN'T GIVE WHAT YOU DON'T HAVE

During that time of relaxation, reflection, and revival, it became clear that was exactly what I was doing! Here I had been trying to feed others while not allowing God to feed me. I was suffering from spiritual anorexia. Even now, I remember an old gospel song I used to hear the choir sing at the Mount Moriah Baptist Church in Los Angeles: "Fill my cup, fill it up and make me whole!" [1] I needed filling and I needed it fast.

Something had to be done! A refocus and retooling had to take place! A reexamination of my life, my heart, my faith, and my mind had to happen! I had to get back on track. So I resolved, then and there, that prayer had to be at the center of everything, including my ministry—yes, even my ministry! Funny that a preacher had to make that decision, but that was where I was in a dark and dramatic time of my life. It was during that time of prayer that God did what God does—God helps us see who we are in relation to God and reminds us that we are not all alone. All of our help comes from the Lord.

PRAYER ALLOWS GOD TO DO SOMETHING WITH YOU

After spending several days with my friend and brother, the Lord began to restore my life and renew my spirit for ministry. It was as if the Twenty-third Psalm came alive for me once again. "You have bedded me down in lush meadows, / you find me quiet pools to drink from. / True to your word, / you let me catch my breath / and send me in the right direction" (Psalm 23:2-3 *Message*). It was at this point that I discovered prayer is *not* God doing something *for* us; prayer is not God becoming a spiritual, cosmic bellhop to entertain our whims and desires; prayer is *not* rubbing on a magic lamp or bottle and out pops a miracle at our request; but prayer is allowing God to do something *with* me, my life, and my ministry, and the church, God's church! Prayer causes us to look up to God, who is seen and who then becomes the source of our strength for abundant life and ministry.

God gave me a new lease on life and ministry through the power of prayer. Developing a personal time of prayer and devotion became a pressing priority; but it also became more. Prayer became a lifestyle, essential to my spiritual survival. The power of prayer began to teach that this is not petty, human business—this is God's business! It is not dependent upon us, but it is dependent upon God. Prayer, then, takes a load off of our shoulders because we now know that we are not carrying this load alone. Jesus bears the yoke; we simply walk beside him obediently. It makes us, as Dr. Zan Holmes would preach, "Check our egos at the door!" Once again, the vernacular of the elderly members of the church while I was growing up came to mind and reminded me that, "Prayer is the key to the kingdom and faith unlocks the door." Wow! That experience taught me something about prayer that I had long overlooked. Prayer is a lifestyle and not just a certain moment in the day or evening. We breathe prayer. We live prayer. We move in the power of prayer. We operate through prayer. Our ministries should be the product of prayer. Our lives should be a reflection of prayer!

The importance of prayer, fasting, Scripture reading, and other spiritual disciplines once again became a part of my spiritual diet. They had to, if I wanted to continue to grow as a spiritual leader of God's people. They have to be, if you want to be a spiritual leader of God's people. We must all learn that we cannot give what we don't have. We cannot put out what we have not taken in. So often we preachers, pastors, and spiritual leaders try to go it alone and do it by ourselves. But we cannot do God's business without God's power! God's power is unleashed through us and works through us only as we are connected to our spiritual source, which comes through prayer, the Word, worship, and the practice of the spiritual disciplines. Prayer brought me back! Prayer refocused me! Prayer centered me! This experience taught me that what we do, we do not in our own power and strength, but through the power of God. That power is available to us and unleashed through us in prayer.

GOD WILL EQUIP YOU WITH POWER

From that point on, I began to reorganize every ministry around prayer, and it began a journey that teaches the very aspects of prayer in the life of the spiritual leader, the leadership, and the congregation and its ministries. Before my crisis I knew Jesus' admonishment, and Paul's, that we should pray without ceasing, but it baffled me. How does one stay in a constant state of prayer? Does that mean we stay on our knees or at someone's altar at all times? How can we stay in a perpetual state of communion with the holy and go about our everyday routines, ministries, and lives? What does it mean to always pray or pray without ceasing? Then it hit me, prayer is not something we do—prayer is who we are! There might be designated times of prayer, but it must go further and deeper than that. Prayer shapes our lives and penetrates our thought processes; it informs our decisions, influences our conduct, and inspires our actions.

Prayer is not a magical incantation that opens up heaven and gets God to do what we want God to do! Prayer is not our route to easy money, success, fame, or acclaim. Don't get me wrong. I do believe God can move in powerful and miraculous ways when we pray. But even if God moves in ways I may not want, I still believe in the power of prayer. Prayer is not designed to get God to do what we want; rather, prayer empowers us to do what God wants. Prayer is not for God; prayer is for us! It helps us stay connected to the power source of our ministry and the power source of the church. Prayer is the connection between ourselves and the holy so that God can move *us* in ways that we did not know we could be moved. God empowers us to do things we once thought were impossible to accomplish! In prayer, not only do we hear the words of the angel Gabriel to Mary, "For nothing will be impossible with God" (Luke 1:37). We are also able to respond as Mary, "Here am I, the servant of the Lord; let it be with me according to your word." (Luke 1:38). Through prayer, we not only see God at work in the world; we allow God to be at work in us!

PRAYER IS A LIFESTYLE

Prayer is a lifestyle inspired, informed, and directed by the Holy Spirit to do God's will upon this Earth through us and with us. Prayer moves the church and its ministries to be in line with God's purposes for that particular place. When prayer becomes the lifestyle of individuals and the church rather than simply a set-aside time or a particular ministry that tells God everything God already knows, we then learn to pray without ceasing. Our lives become our time of prayer. We begin to see God's power unleashed in the congregation and in the life of the pastor and leadership. Through prayer we become *focused* on our mission, clear in our vision, and undying to our commitment to the gospel of Jesus Christ. When a church's very foundation for ministry is prayer, a new spirit takes shape. The church births new life and a new sense of optimism—even more, a strong faith takes hold! A church that bathes all it does in prayer is an exciting church. It is a church that can't wait to see what God is about to do next in its midst. A praying church is a church that does not depend on itself, its name, or its buildings and budgets to get ministry done; rather, it depends on the power of God that is at work among the people who are busy doing what God has called the church to do.

PRAYER EMPOWERS YOU TO LIVE FOR GOD

Prayer is the very lifeblood of the pastor and congregation as we together commune with the God of heaven and are empowered to live out the gospel in ways that make God known on Earth through our words and deeds. The power of prayer keeps the ministry F.O.C.U.S. within the church and its leadership. It helps us live by the power of prayer and not just say our prayers. There is a difference!

There is power when God's people live prayer and not just say their prayers. Therefore, we are invited by Christ to grow into a life of prayer. The disciples seemed to grasp this concept as they watched the power of Christ unfold and be displayed in his preaching, teaching, his love, and his miracles! Jesus did not just say "his" prayers; he lived a life of prayer. Everything he did was done because he stayed connected with God, not just for an hour or two a day, but without ceasing! No wonder the disciples asked in Luke 11:1, "Lord, teach us to pray." Teach us, Lord, to live with the same power that you have! Teach us, Lord, to be in constant communion with

God, who in turn will help us be in a dynamic relationship with one another and the world around us. Teach us to be and stay connected! That was the opening Jesus needed to introduce us to what we know as the Lord's Prayer.

My journey taught me that the Lord's Prayer is key to living a *focused* life of prayer. It gives us the ingredients for a prayerful lifestyle, one that relies on God, works for God, enhances the kingdom of God, and is guided and protected by God! This gives us the pattern of a prayer-*full* life! It has in it the ingredients for a powerful witness to the world through spiritual leadership in and through the local church. It is a powerful church that sees its standards for living, giving, and witness in the Lord's Prayer! It is a church and pastor with F.O.C.U.S.!

F.O.C.U.S. calls us to be Faithful, Open, Centered, United, and Solid in our mission, vision, commitment, witness, and discipleship. This book will help you learn the lifestyle of prayer by studying the prayer that Jesus taught us. Through living the Lord's Prayer, a congregation will find itself on the cutting edge of ministry and proclaiming a relevant gospel in this contemporary world. A spiritual leader will find renewal and refreshment.

Let us pray. I mean, let us live in the manner that Jesus taught us! I can hear Jesus say, "When you pray or as you live, say..."

QUESTIONS FOR REFLECTION

1. Share a time when you needed God.

2. What do you want God to teach you about prayer?

3. Who is someone you know who lives a lifestyle of prayer?

4. Where do you need God to equip you with power?

5. How is God moving in your church today?

6. If God unleashed more power for love and service in your church, how would it be different? How would you be different?

F.O.C.U.S.—FAITHFUL TO GOD!

Our Father in heaven, hallowed be your name.
—Matthew 6:9

W e pray not to get God's attention, but so that God can get our attention. Prayer is our interaction and dialogue with the God of the universe. So often we have made prayer a monologue where we do all the talking and presume God does all the listening. In this view, God takes our orders and responds when we get ready for God to respond. This treats God as though God is a cashier at a spiritual drive-through restaurant. That is not prayer at all! Prayer is a dialogue between ourselves and God, a time when God hears us, but more important, a time when we listen to God. Even more so, prayer is best when we get up off of our knees and live in its power. That is when prayer becomes a lifestyle.

FOCUS ON GOD'S WILL AND GOD'S WAY

As we live out the Lord's Prayer in its fullness in our lives and through our ministries in the church, it becomes clear who is in charge! As we begin in faith, it becomes clear to us who the focus is: God—God's will and God's way. After all, it is the Lord's church and not our church! It is the Lord's agenda and not our agenda! When we are clear on who we are and whose we are, we come before the Lord without any agendas because the focus is on God and not on us.

When God is the focus, we can better resist the temptation to make prayer an outline or wish list, but rather a time of total surrender and submission as we give ourselves to God's will—for God's work—to build God's kingdom. The Lord's Prayer places the focus on God so that we can learn to be faithful to the God who calls us in the first place. Jesus taught us that this is God's business and not ours! It is about God and not us! Jesus said, "On this rock I will build my church, and the gates of Hades will not prevail against it" (Matthew 16:18). God's church is built on a secure and solid foundation. Nothing can destroy or uproot it. Waves of doubt, apathy, hate, or ineffective ministry can't wash it away. This is something we all must be reminded of from time to time.

The burnout experience I mentioned in the previous chapter taught me that there are times we get ahead of God. Sometimes we think we can function on our own and sustain ourselves by our own power. That is a lie from hell! We cannot do this on our own. Living the Lord's Prayer helps us come to grips with the reality of our limited abilities and God's unlimited power! This is God's doing and God is faithful to bring to pass what we in faith place in God's hands. One passage of Scripture that keeps me together when it feels as though the ministry load is too heavy and about to unravel is Philippians 1:6. The Apostle Paul says, "I am confident of this, that the one who began a good work among you will bring it to completion by the day of Jesus Christ." It reminds us that God, through Jesus Christ, has assumed responsibility to empower us to ensure that king-dom building proceeds, often in spite of us!

Living the Lord's Prayer places the focus in the right place as it all begins and ends with God. "Our Father in heaven, hallowed be your name!" The dreams, the vision for the church, its ministries, its witness, its outreach, its worship, and even its growth all begin with God! This real-ization causes us to submit to God's dreams and place our dreams on the back burner; and God, through the Holy Spirit, will give us the wisdom to distinguish between the two. God's vision is the preferred future for the church! When we begin with God, we begin with inspiration and direction that has been inspired by God; and is directed by God. God breathed and God ordained.

When I was in a prayerful quandary of making a decision to leave the Saint Mark Church in Wichita to accept the appointment of the St. Luke "Community" United Methodist Church in Dallas in 2002, I had a conversation with Bishop Dick Wills (of course, this was before his elec-tion to the episcopacy). I was fearful of the change. I was afraid of leaving a place where I had grown quite comfort-able. I was scared to move from a church I watched grow and blossom to become one of the largest churches in our United Methodist connection. Even worse, I was petrified to follow in the footsteps of the legendary Dr. Zan Wesley Holmes, Jr.! Bishop Wills took me outside of our meeting in Nashville and talked with me for over an hour, and then he prayed with me. I shall never forget that prayer and will always respect and love him for what he did for me that day. He said, "Lord, I am not asking you to open any doors for Tyrone, but I am asking that you close all doors so that he will know what door to walk in!" That was awesome! It put the Lord, the Lord's will, and the Lord's way first and placed my desires and will on the back burner. Frequently Bishop

Wills has noted how we want God to bless and sanction what we are doing, when we should be asking the Lord to take us and allow us to participate in what the Lord is already blessing.

FOCUS ON THE LORD'S DOING

We lose our focus and our grounding when we take God out of God's rightful place in our lives and in the church. As I have stated previously, this is the Lord's church. This is the Lord's doing. This is the Lord's blessing upon us. I messed up big-time when I started thinking in an arrogant way that this was Tyrone's doing and even worse, this was Tyrone's church. What a slippery slope we build with that arrogant and sinful philosophy. The Lord's Prayer points us to the One who is leading and guiding the church and who reminds us that every good and perfect gift comes from above! That is why Jesus teaches the prayer beginning with, "Our Father who is in heaven, hallowed be your name!"

Any major decisions the church undertakes or makes concerning ministry direction should always be undergirded with prayer, and sometimes fasting! If we truly believe this is God's doing (and it is); and that this is the Lord's church (which it is), then we certainly need to be taking situations and decisions to God to help us discern God's way and God's will. There are times when we must make major decisions on the direction of the church, staffing, building, and financing, and even major conflict. In our church, we came to the conclusion that we could not make decisions just by voting. First we needed to do some serious praying! During these times we would schedule prayer vigils with the leadership and congregation. Sometimes we would be in prayer all night and would even designate the day as a day of fasting for those who physically were able to participate. In prayer, we are putting God first by seeking God's direction for God's church. I am telling you, the whole congregation sees and experiences God's power in dramatic yet peaceful ways.

There was even a time when we were having issues with a disgruntled staff member. When the staff member left, there was some resentment, both on the part of that person and with some members in the church. Emails were sent out and caused divisions within the community of faith. We called a prayer meeting on a Wednesday night, praying for the peace and unity of the church. I opened it up by addressing some of the major issues and answering some questions but refusing to get down and dirty about the situation. I just believe things should be done right and above-board. Some things were private and others were personnel matters. These issues had already been addressed fully in the proper venue, which was with the Pastor-Parish Relations Committee, the district superintendent, and the bishop. I simply refused to put that person's personal business out there like that!

In my heart, I did not believe dragging someone else through the mud would solve anything except get us all dirty, myself included. Maybe that is why I love a line in the gospel hymn by Charles Albert Tindley, "Beams of Heaven," which says: "There is a God that rules above; with hand of power and a heart of love; / and if I am right, he'll fight my battle." Let me tell you, we prayed and prayed and placed the situation in God's hands, and God worked! I learned as a teenager from my late pastor, the Reverend Earl Pleasant, in Los Angeles that God honors faithfulness. I believe that to be true. When we are faithful in taking care of God's business by placing God first, God will take care of us.

On another occasion, in Wichita, Saint Mark was grow-ing by leaps and bounds, the sanctuary was overflowing to the point when persons had to stand around the walls for the service—for a two-hour African American worship celebra-tion that was no small feat! Then a controversy arose. A doc-trinal controversy on the role of the Holy Spirit, speaking in tongues, and being baptized in the Trinitarian formula or in Jesus' name only. When churches grow as we did, that kind of "stuff" will happen. Recognizing that this was the Lord's church and seeking God's direction on how to deal with an issue that could potentially cause a major division in the church, a group of leaders came to pray along with me and deal with the issue. Through prayer, it became apparent that a sermon series on the work of the Holy Spirit as understood in the Wesleyan tradition was needed to confront some of the major parties involved. That was a difficult time and a difficult challenge that was once again causing me to lose focus. I was forgetting whose church this really was; I thought it would tear up "my church"! I had to be reminded by some dedicated laity, "Pastor G., we have given this over to the Lord! This is the Lord's church and not our church, so we must do what needs to be done, and God has our backs!"

I shall never forget, after the second sermon in the series, an Anglo woman, whom I had seen visiting for several Sundays before and never saw again after this encounter, came up to me after worship and said, "God has this under control! You preach the word and you make sure you are obedient to God's will, and God will do the rest! You will lose some in the midst of this but the coming harvest will be even greater!" That blew my mind! Over the next couple of months, what she said would happen—happened! We lost some folks over this, but afterward, the harvest was greater than the loss. In fact, we had to build a new facility to han-dle the great harvest and increase God placed in our hands.

Church attendance tripled in size. Putting God first, staying faithful to God's call on one's ministry, and God's call on the church are the first steps to living the Lord's Prayer.

To underscore this even more and to keep this before us at all times, I have adopted the practice of leaving the head chair at staff meetings and church council meetings empty. No one sits in that chair. That is Jesus' seat. It reminds us who the Chair really is. It reminds us who really is in charge. Whenever we vote or make decisions or get into discussions, we can't help but see that empty seat and know that the Lord is with us and is guiding us in all we do. That is our way of making sure the Lord is first and that we stay faithful to God.

FOCUS ON DOING GOD'S NEW THING

The Lord's Prayer helps us live faithfully to our calling as disciples of Jesus Christ and be faithful as the Lord's church. We live this out by constantly seeking God's will for the life of the church. God is ever moving and God, as the prophet Isaiah declares, is always doing a new thing (43:19). As my good friend Dr. Joseph Daniels, senior pastor of the Emory United Methodist Church in Washington, D.C., says, "Do first things first and second things not at all." That is what putting God first and being faithful to our call will do. It helps us prioritize. God did not call all persons or churches to do all things. God has a place for each of us, work for each of us, and a part of the vineyard for each of us in which to minister.

Living out the very first line of the Lord's Prayer helped me realize that God gave each church and each ministry its own fingerprints. As human beings, we have our own distinct fingerprints—so does each church. We all have the same mission—to make disciples for Jesus Christ, but we go

about it in different ways. We have our distinct ways, per-
sonalities, and callings to present the gospel in culturally
relevant ways in these contemporary times. When God,
rather than our own ambitions, is first, God reveals what
that distinctiveness is.

As God remains first and foremost in our ministries, and
as churches we live out our faithfulness to our calling, we
are living out the Lord's Prayer! "Our Father, who is in
heaven, hallowed be your name." Lord, you are first in all
we say and do. Lord, this is your thing. Lord, you gave birth
to the church. Lord, you empower your church. Lord, you
called your church. Lord, you give your church vision and
purpose. In our decisions, you are first. In our ministries, you
are first. In our lives, you are first. In our policy making, you
are first. In our giving, you are first. In our loving, you are
first. In our witnessing, you are first. By staying faithful to
God, we are making the Lord number one in all we do and
say. The Word once again becomes flesh and dwells among
us and brings light in the midst of darkness and despair.

FOCUS ON LIVING YOUR PRAYERS

The Lord's Prayer is not merely a beautiful set of words to
be recited at the altar, or during the Communion ritual, or
at night before we retire; it is a model and standard by
which we are expected to live, operate, and practice ministry. I don't think Jesus taught this to be simply a prayer to
be said, but a prayer to be lived. Jesus teaches us this prayer
so we can become active participants in kingdom building
and living. It becomes the standard and the model of our
behavior as the community of faith and as its spiritual leaders. It reminds us that it is not about us; but it is all about
God.

"Lord, teach us to pray," the disciples requested. Yet, instead of teaching them to pray words, Jesus taught them how to live as his disciples. The first step of our FOCUS as disciples as we live the Lord's Prayer is staying faithful to God! God is first, and everything we do must revolve around that fact. We are true to God when we are true to the calling and purpose God has placed on our lives and our ministries. We don't have to be anyone else and we don't have to be like anyone else. As we are faithful to God and ourselves, then whatever we ask in the Lord's name will be done. Now we are ready to roll up our sleeves and make it happen in the world as we pray that his kingdom come.

QUESTIONS FOR REFLECTION

1. How might your life be different if you focused on God more?

2. Where in your life have you experienced God's calling? How do you plan to live out that calling?

3. What dreams do you have for your life, the life of your family, the life of your church, the life of your community?

4. What might be God's dream for your life, your family, your church, your community?

5. What might be some distractions or obstacles that keep you from focusing on God and God's dreams?

6. How can we change to live into God's dreams for our lives, families, churches, and communities?

F.O.C.U.S.—OPEN TO THE OPPORTUNITIES

Your kingdom come. / Your will be done, / on earth as it is in heaven. —Matthew 6:10

What a powerful and meaningful statement! No matter how good or well-meaning it sounds, we cannot do this kind of kingdom work without the aid of kingdom power. We cannot do this by ourselves. We have a tendency to want what we want, when we want it, and how we want it. It is so easy to place our will above God's will and our agendas above God's kingdom, but when we make prayer a lifestyle, it becomes easier and easier to not only pray this prayer but also to live this prayer.

LIVING IN OPENNESS TO THE HOLY SPIRIT

The power we need to live a kingdom lifestyle is unleashed in us through the power of prayer. Prayer is the vehicle through which the Holy Spirit moves us, operates through us, and motivates and activates us to be about

God's work. We could not really pray like this without the Holy Spirit's power and influence in our lives. As we live a lifestyle of prayer, the Holy Spirit guides us toward a multitude of opportunities where we can be a prophetic witness and an advocate for the standards and goals of the kingdom of God. Without openness to God's fresh movements, we will ultimately become stagnant, stale, and sour in our ministries and in the church. We then become more concerned and preoccupied with *church work* instead of the *work of the church*! I believe *church work* is operating within the realm of a maintenance ministry mentality while *the work of the church* is having a mission-minded ministry. One oils the machinery of the church while the other drives the mission of the church. I believe the deaths of so many churches and ministries come about because of a preoccupation with church work to the neglect of the church's service and work in the community and world. We often major in the minors and minor in the majors. However, we regain our focus by not simply praying this prayer but by living this prayer: "Your kingdom come, your will be done, on earth as it is in heaven."

Openness to Walking in Faith

As we live this prayer, God is challenging us to move out of our comfort zones and take risks of faith so that others might experience the transforming, liberating, and saving power of the kingdom of God in their lives and in our society. The whole point of God sending Jesus was for change— to change the world, to change us. God is still changing the world and using us to bring about that change; that is what Jesus is teaching us in the model prayer. Bishop Desmond Tutu, who experienced firsthand the ugly, inhumane treatment of human beings to one another in South Africa, writes of this hope and faith and work of the Christian community. Bishop Tutu writes: "If God is transfiguring the world, you may ask, why does [God] need our help? The answer is quite simple: we are the agents of transformation that God uses to transfigure [God's] world."[1]

"Your kingdom come, your will be done, on earth as it is in heaven." God uses us because we are God's hands, God's feet, God's eyes! We feel with the heart of God and speak with the mouth of God. God gives us the opportunities to make God's kingdom known in the midst of the pains, hurts, and brokenness of our world. That is why we must stay open to the opportunities to make God's will known on earth as it is in heaven.

OPENNESS TO KINGDOM POSSIBILITIES

This statement requires that we don't just pray for God's will to be done and that God's kingdom fills this Earth, but we also work through our lives and ministry toward that end. This is the goal of ministry and the church, that the world gets a glimpse of the kingdom of God in our lives, our ministries, our mission, and our churches. Living this out means we stay open to new opportunities to live out the gospel in word and deed. This lifestyle of the kingdom continuously breaks down barriers of separation that keep the kingdom and its goals at a distance as a mere ideal instead of a reality.

The model prayer as an example of the model life of a disciple of Christ guides our ministries and challenges us to remain open to the opportunities of the kingdom it presents. I have discovered with God, there are always new opportunities and unlimited possibilities to be in ministry to our communities and the world! I vividly recall driving to the church office one morning and sitting at a stoplight at a busy intersection in Wichita. Being preoccupied with other thoughts, I happened to look up at the advertisement of a pawnshop in the community. What I saw disturbed me deeply. In big and bold wording it said, *"Uzis for sale!"* Uzis? What in the world is going on? Who would buy that particular gun except a drug dealer or a gangbanger? We had to make a statement as the body of Christ! We had to let the pawnshop know that we were not standing for this! The ad ran counter to the goals of God's kingdom of peace in our community. To make a long story short, we wrote and called the media! The pawnshop owners were stubborn and refused to be intimidated by a church. However, they had no idea they were running up against a church that believed in living and operating by the principles of the Lord's Prayer. We made it known in no uncertain terms that we would not stand for this and would march, protest, and do whatever else needed to be done to get that sign changed. We won the standoff! In fact, the pawnshop had to eventually move because we were not going to have them perpetrate the violence we as a community were trying to eradicate. The Lord's Prayer informs us and causes us to take an unpopular stand on sometimes polarizing issues. But when we are on God's side we have power to stand!

God is always doing something new, providing new and inspiring new venues through which we live out the gospel. The Lord is calling us to launch out into the deep waters of ministry and mission and come out of the shallow waters of self-centeredness, materialism, false piety, and a maintenance ministry. This model prayer merely consists of words on a page if we refuse to stay fresh and open to new moves of God so that they become life through our lives, ministries, and churches. We fail the test as we become isolated in our own little worlds, ministries, outlook, mission, and outreach. These words lose their meaning when we are more concerned about caring for the needs on the inside of the church and forget the needs in the community outside of our stained glass windows.

Ministry isolation causes us to close the door on what God is doing and keeps us numb to the hurts, the evil, and the sin that is all around us. Staying open to the opportunities that God provides keeps us relevant, prophetic witnesses in the world. When we close the doors on God's opportunities to live out the Lord's Prayer, we will become irrelevant and obsolete, having no meaning or a fresh word for those who desperately need it. Our ministries, our worship, and our churches become irrelevant. Our preaching becomes irrelevant! Our mission becomes irrelevant! We become obsessed with maintaining the status quo and oiling the machinery of the church instead of being on the forefront of doing God's will and making the kingdom of God real for those who have to deal with the kingdom of the devil every day of their lives. We miss out on so many opportunities because we are narrow-minded and tightfisted, becoming narrow in our outreach and constricted in our mission! The Lord's Prayer calls for us to be open to God's new opportunities to make God's will, love, grace, and justice known through us and through the church to the world.

In August of 1988, I went to Wichita for my Introductory Interview at Saint Mark as pastor with the Pastor-Parish Relations Committee. Along with the Wichita district superintendent, Marsha and I walked into the fellowship hall of the church, which was packed with folks who wanted to see and hear the new preacher. Keep in mind, a Pastor-Parish Relations Committee has only nine members, but there had to be almost fifty people crowded into that room! Most faces were friendly, but others were not. How intimidating this was to a young preacher coming into a strange and new place! I shall never forget a question asked of me, "What do you expect to happen *if* you become the pastor of Saint Mark?" Well, the "if" caught my ear quickly, but my sense of expectation got me more. I simply said, "I expect someone to walk down these aisles every Sunday and make a commitment to Jesus Christ!" Then a smug response came from a corner, "Well, good luck, preacher!" There was no sense of expectation of what could happen when we open ourselves up to God's opportunities.

OPENNESS TO THE UNEXPECTED WAYS OF GOD

To have any sense of expectation, we must be open to what I call divine opportunities, to be in ministry and witness in new and creative ways! That made me even more aware of the fact that God moves in unexpected ways and we must live with a sense of wonder and expectation of the opportunities God will provide for us to make a difference in the world.

My first week there, I began to dream God's dreams for my ministry and that church. I wanted God's kingdom to become real for so many persons who had given up on God, on life, the community, and the church. I wanted to be open for what God had in store. I wanted to be open to the new opportunities of ministry. I wanted to be a part of what God was going to do. I stood there on the property, which at the time was nothing but land and a little church building, and declared in faith, "Lord, one day you will make this place become a place of possibilities and transformation!" In other words, this will be a place that will stay open to the opportunities to make the kingdom known through words and deeds. This will be a place where God's opportunities to be in ministry will be accepted! This will be a place that will be open to God's movements and God's directions to do ministry in new and creative ways. I wanted to be a part of a ministry and a community of faith that lived the model prayer and didn't just pray it on Sunday morning.

God is a God of possibilities and new opportunities! As we live out the model prayer, we must be sensitive to how God is moving in the world around us. We must be ever vigilant in seeking God's will and living that out in places and among lives that are out of sync with God's will. "Your kingdom come, your will be done, on earth as it is in heaven" is a statement of action. It denotes a kingdom-building lifestyle and a call to churches to have kingdom-building ministries! It means we must stay fresh, relevant, open, and on the cutting edge.

What I love about St. Luke "Community" United Methodist Church is that we are clear about the balance between the living presence of the gospel of Jesus Christ within the lives of disciples and the ministry of the church. That balance reminds us that a spiritual relationship with God has social dimensions. Therefore, St. Luke embodies the fact that the model prayer is not simply a prayer to be prayed but a prayer to be lived! St. Luke has always seen itself as a "cross-shaped" church. We see ourselves as a church that "reaches up to God and out into the 'community!'" It is embedded in everything we say and do. It's portrayed on our logo It's a part of our mission. It is the main component of our vision for the future. It is made perfectly clear in our core values. It is even found in our welcome song, written by our Minister of Worship and the Arts, Ms. Monya Davis Logan! Every Sunday we greet our guests by singing, "Welcome to 'the Luke,' where Jesus is Lord! Welcome to 'the Luke,' where we make a joyful noise! We are the church that reaches up to God! We are the church that reaches out to everyone! Welcome, welcome, welcome to 'the Luke!'" These are simple but effective things any church can do to make real their efforts to live the Lord's Prayer.

To remind ourselves to be open to the opportunities to make God's kingdom known and real in a world that is skeptical and sidetracked, we review our mission and vision statements before any ministry begins its meetings. We also incorporate it in our worship liturgy monthly and have posted it throughout the campuses of our church. Our mission is: "We are a community of God's caring people, where the gospel of Jesus Christ is proclaimed, disciples are made, and lives are transformed, equipped, and empowered by the Holy Spirit to bring liberation throughout the community and world." Our vision, which points to where we see God leading us, is: "We believe God is calling us through the Holy Spirit, to a ministry of excellence, that seeks to reach all persons by providing a warm and loving Christian atmosphere, where children, youth, adults, and families are nurtured and equipped to reach their God-given potential; to be an advocate for community empowerment; and a prophetic voice for all oppressed peoples with love, grace, and justice as our guiding force" (see appendix). It all points to making the kingdom known on earth as it is in heaven.

OPENNESS TO WEEKDAY ACTIVISM

We are not content with just being a worshiping church that only lifts holy hands to God on Sunday; rather, we are a working, disciple-making, transforming community that reaches its hands out into the world on Monday. We strive to be a church that has the ability to take the inspiration of Sunday and turn it into activism on Monday by making the kingdom a little clearer and nearer on Earth as it is in heaven. Through our ministries, actions, and mission we are living the model prayer, "Your kingdom come, your will be done, on earth as it is in heaven." God has given us the opportunity to continue the mission of Jesus in the world. He made that clear through his inaugural sermon, found in Luke 4:18-19:

> "The Spirit of the Lord is upon me,
>   because he has anointed me
>   to bring good news to the
>   poor.
> He has sent me to proclaim release to the
>   captives
>   and recovery of sight to the blind,
>   to let the oppressed go free,
> to proclaim the year of the Lord's favor."

OPENNESS TO MAKING BOLD DECISIONS

To have a prayer-filled and empowered life and ministry mean we must make some bold decisions and proclamations of what this means. We cannot just simply ask God to do something that we are not willing to join in and partner with God to accomplish. Nor can we simply pray and sit back doing nothing and naively expecting God to do it all. That is not prayer; that is magic. If we are praying for the kingdom to come and God's will to be done—then by the power of God what are we doing to make it happen? Are we just muttering words or are we willing to put our request into action?

There are many implications and risks that we take when we stand in agreement with God to stay open to the opportunities to make God's kingdom and will known in the world. This line of the model prayer not only has spiritual undertones but also speaks to our social responsibility in the world! This prayer refuses to allow us to compartmentalize and adhere to the popular religious ideas that there is a separation between the spiritual and the social. Such a separation is not biblical! Our relationship with God has social implications. We cannot live the Lord's Prayer and stay held up in the comforts of our safe sanctuaries and beautiful buildings. It forces us to be a force of faith that must be reckoned with in the world. It will force us to be a prophetic voice for the marginalized, the dispossessed, the oppressed, and the outcast. "Your kingdom come, your will be done, on earth as it is in heaven."

OPENNESS TO LOVING THE WORLD

In other words, whatever we believe is going on in heaven or what heaven is like—we move and work towards that end on Earth! This prayer will not allow our churches, our ministries, or our lives to be so heavenly minded that we are of no earthly good! The model prayer causes us to switch our focus from the *sweet bye and bye* and help folks live and survive in the *nasty now and now*! It keeps us focused and opened to the opportunities of kingdom building in a world that is in opposition to the values of the kingdom of God! With our lives and our ministries we live out this prayer to make a difference in the lives of others. This prayer will call into question all that is not of God and empower God's children to work for that kingdom that will have no end!

If all of God's children "got" shoes in heaven, as an African American spiritual says, then we ought to make sure all of God's children have shoes on their feet on Earth! If all of God's children have a robe in heaven, then we ought to make sure all of God's children are clothed here on Earth! If we have a mansion in heaven, then we ought to make sure that all of God's children have affordable housing here on Earth! If there is no sickness in heaven, then we ought to be on the forefront of fighting to make sure all of God's children have access to adequate health care on Earth! "Your kingdom come, your will be done, on earth as it is in heaven."

God is at work even now in the world, doing a work through us and with us. Therefore, we must be focused on being open to the opportunities provided to us by the God who loves the world! In a world of hate, strife, war, bigotry, poverty, and destruction, people need a glimpse of the kingdom. If they don't get a glimpse of it through us in the church, then where will it take place? If they cannot see it now, then when will it become apparent? The time is now to tear Satan's kingdom down and build God's kingdom up! God has opened many doors of opportunity for us to be in ministry and witness to make disciples and proclaim this gospel in word and deed. Since God has opened the doors— we must be open to the opportunities. Are we willing to be a witness? "Your kingdom come, your will be done, on earth as it is in heaven."

QUESTIONS FOR REFLECTION

1. Tell of a time when you experienced God in a powerful way.

2. Who do you know who is open to God?

3. What step of faith would you like to take now?

4. How can you be more open to serving God and others?

5. How can you and your faith community make the kingdom real to those around you?

6. How does your church reflect its openness to God?

7. What are you working toward in your faith?

8. Where in your life do you need God?

9. Where does your community need God? What do you want to do about it?

F.O.C.U.S.—Centered
on Commitment
to Faith

Give us this day our daily bread. —Matthew 6:11

Give us this day our daily bread" is a call to live a life of faith, trust, and dependence upon God. It is a call to trust that God will provide for the needs of our lives, our ministries, and our churches. It is also a call to be God's vehicle and conduit of blessings so that the needs of those who have not are met as well.

Living the Lord's Prayer is a challenge because it is a journey of faith in all aspects. Of course, this is not blind faith but a faith that is focused, centered, and reliant on God's guidance. It is a life that gets up every day, trusting in the new and fresh mercies of God and placing everything in the hands of our faithful God. While this is good "church talk," putting it into action is a daily challenge. Why? Because of our human tendency to want to be in control and in charge of everything! We just have a need to have our hands in everything instead of placing everything in the hands of God. As we live the model prayer, we are called to live our lives centered on a commitment of faith.

CENTERED IN A TEACHABLE MOMENT

In this *teachable moment* when Jesus spoke this prayer to his disciples, their minds must have traced back to their people's historic forty-year wandering in the wilderness after their miraculous emancipation and liberation from slavery in Egypt. The story is found in Exodus 16. After a time, the food ran out, and the wilderness in all its barrenness yielded nothing to eat. The people of course grumbled and complained, as we church people sometimes like to do when things appear to be running low! But then God said to Moses in Exodus 16:4, "I am going to rain bread from heaven for you, and each day the people shall go out and gather enough for that day. In that way I will test them, whether they will follow my instruction or not." The key phrase is "gather enough for that day." That was a test to see if they could learn to depend and trust God daily for their physical sustenance and nourishment. Every morning God provided them the breadlike substance called *manna*, which in Hebrew means "what is it?" What they lacked, God provided! It was God dependably caring for them.

The command was to take only what was needed for that day and not store up or hoard for themselves because that would be a sign of distrust in God's promise of daily provisions. So every morning, for forty years, God provided their daily bread! Every morning new mercies of God were experienced. Every morning what they needed, God's hand provided. Every morning they experienced the care of a loving God. God's faithfulness was experienced and they had the opportunity to learn about faith in the God who does all things well. From that image and history Jesus says to us that when we pray we should also say, "Give us this day our daily bread."

Like the disciples, we constantly need teachable moments of faith so that we grow in our daily trust and dependence upon God to guide, care, sustain, and provide for us. "Give us this day our daily bread" is a reminder that God is our Sustainer and our Provider! It is an acknowledgment that we are not in charge or in control, but God is! It is a daily affirmation in which we recognize it is in God we move, we live, and have our being! It is a call to trust God for what we need for life in order to do what must be done in life!

CENTERED ON BEING A DAILY BLESSING

It is also a reminder that we are blessed to be a daily blessing to others. Instead of selfishly hoarding what we have, we give so others might live! There are others in the world who depend on God to provide for their needs through us. This is one of the reasons this great hymn of the church speaks so succinctly and poignantly to me:

> Guide me, O thou Great Jehovah, pilgrim through this barren land.
> I am weak, but thou art mighty; hold me with thy powerful hand.
> Bread of heaven, bread of heaven, feed me till I want no more.

What would it be like if God fed the world until there was no more hunger? How might this play out in a world filled with poverty, hunger, and greed? How could this be lived out in a society where many of our senior citizens must decide between *daily bread* and *daily meds*? Our prayers should be urgent and expectant in a world where we constantly see children's bloated bellies on our TV screens. What would our churches be like if we were faithful to

God's promise to give daily bread? How would our nation, the richest in the world, be different if we faithfully fed the poor? God gives to us so that we can give to others. God, as I said earlier, blesses us to be a blessing. Even if most of the world's wealth is controlled by a small percentage of people, we know that it is God who provides. We should not be bothered by our own lack of resources, because we know that we may be weak, but God is strong. If we as Christians and churches throughout the world truly lived this prayer, our hearts would go out to ensure that the needs of others anywhere and everywhere are met.

During the horrific aftermath of Hurricane Katrina, it was a joy to see St. Luke "Community" United Methodist Church living this prayer out as thousands of evacuees con-verged upon Dallas for relief and help during their tragic time of suffering, devastation, and loss. Across the street from our Community Life Center is a city park that was set up as a relief center. But there were no showers and no food for the evacuees coming; it was a sight to see. One of our staff members, Linda White, saw this and just said, "Why don't we invite them over to the Community Life Center and feed them?" God had given us our daily bread and now it was God who would use St. Luke to ensure others had theirs as well! That immediately began a new ministry at St. Luke without any votes or study committees; it was just someone seeing the need and mobilizing the church to meet it. St. Luke became the relief center for that area, and we received coverage in our city's newspaper and were noted by our United Methodist annual conference. Hundreds of members of St. Luke volunteered their time, restaurants donated food, and churches and businesses throughout the community gave over a hundred thousand dollars to help us live out the Lord's Prayer. Thousands of evacuees received three meals a day, clothing, job training, counseling, help, and housing. This ministry is continuing, even now, as we offer ongoing care for the victims of Hurricane Katrina still in the Dallas area at the time of this writing. To God be the glory!

St. Luke also literally lives this prayer out through two ministries. One is called Loaves and Fishes, a partnership with area churches and the Martin Luther King, Jr., Center in South Dallas, which feeds homeless individuals and families; the other is a partnership with our annual conference called Methodism Breadbasket, which ministers to individuals and families who are having a rough time in their lives. Both ministries help persons rise above their circumstances and work to restore their human dignity by allowing them to look to heaven and say, "Give us this day our daily bread." Both ministries are designed not just to give handouts, but to offer a helping hand! It is called living by faith through the Lord's Prayer.

CENTERED ON DEPENDING AND TRUSTING GOD

Dependence on and trust in God have become religious slogans in so many circles, but hoarding and an obsession with materialism have become the reality of the day. Getting all we *can* and *canning* all we get has become the order of the day. This self-centered philosophy is a direct result of a lack of faith, trust, and nominal dependence on God. It is a modern-day version of a parable told by Jesus in Luke 12:15: " 'Take care! Be on your guard against all kinds of greed; for one's life does not consist in the abundance of possessions.' Then he told them a parable":

> The land of a rich man produced abundantly. And he thought to himself, "What should I do, for I have no place to store my crops?" Then he said, "I will do this: I will pull down my barns

and build larger ones, and there I will store all my grain and my goods. And I will say to my soul, 'Soul, you have ample goods laid up for many years; relax, eat, drink, be merry.'" But God said to him, "You fool! This very night your life is being demanded of you. And the things you have prepared, whose will they be?"(Luke 16:16-20)

The man in the parable only thought of himself and what he had. He gave no thought or consideration to others who stood in need! His success was tied to what he had and not to what he gave. Everything he said and did is contradictory to a life centered on a commitment to live by faith. He loved things more than he loved God. He loved things more than he loved people. He loved things more than he loved the community. This lifestyle is diametrically opposed to what Jesus is teaching us in the model prayer. Not once in this prayer did he mention the poor, the needy, or the have-nots in the world. Not once did he mention any philanthropic activity to help alleviate world hunger, to help some disadvantaged young person fulfill his or her dream to go to college, or to help provide job opportunities to the unemployed in the community so that they could get their daily bread. He lived a foolish lifestyle and not one of faith! A life centered on commitment to faith is a prayerful and prayer-filled life. As we learn to trust and depend on God for our lives, we in turn learn to give our selves, our lives.

Of course when we pray, or shall I say *live*, "Give us this day, our daily bread," we are not simply talking about our physical needs being met. This is a prayer that puts all of life in the hands of God. Give us this day what we need to survive. Give us this day what we need for ministry. Give us this day what we need to overcome the challenges facing us. Give us this day what we need. Give us this day those who we can help. When we live centered on faith, we focus on God's dependability and faithfulness. We can get up each day knowing that nothing will happen to us that God can't handle. It is a faith walk.

While I served the Saint Mark Church in Wichita, we moved from being a fund-raising church to a tithing-and-giving church. That was a journey of faith! That was a step towards asking God to "Give us this day, our daily bread"! Like many churches, Saint Mark struggled to meet its budget, pay its mission and ministry fund to the denomination, and pay for its ministries. Fund-raisers were common activities to supplement the budget. Bake sales, dinners, and the like were held quite often, while teaching a solid lifestyle of stewardship, with *tithing* as its center was secondary. Then the step of faith came. We decided to become a tithing church! We would no longer have these fund-raisers to supplement the budget. That was a step of faith and a great show of trust and dependence upon God to meet the needs of ministry for the church.

After six months, instead of being in the black, we were in the red! We were in the hole. It looked like this biblical principle of giving was not for us. The finance committee met; and as I sat there looking at the numbers, I trembled and waited to see who was going to have the first bake sale or fundraiser to help get us back on track. We discussed—no, to be honest, we argued about what to do. Mind you, one of my top spiritual gifts has always been faith, but it sure was wavering about now! *I* was leading the charge to go back to raising funds like we used to. However, before the vote went forth, Mrs. Cletha Ponds, a woman of great faith, took over the meeting. You need to know that Mrs. Ponds was not the chair, but she became the chair at that moment. I shall never forget that night as she said, "Wait a minute!

What are we doing? We are not going back!" Everybody looked at her as if to say, "Who do you think you are?" She continued by looking at me, the pastor, the spiritual leader, and said, "Pastor, didn't you just preach last Sunday Exodus 14?" I said, "Yes ma'am!" "Didn't you say that the sea didn't open up for the children of Israel until they moved forward?" I responded, "Yes ma'am!" Of course, by then I felt quite embarrassed! She then said, "Maybe we are at our Red Sea and God is testing us to see if we will trust him enough to go forward or will we go back to Egypt. And I don't know about you all, but I am not going back!" After that, dead silence was in the room for several minutes.

We were all convicted by this woman of faith! That for me was a teachable moment. She was saying everything I, as the spiritual leader, should have been saying, but God used her because my faith was wavering. Well, as you would guess, we continued the course and did not go back, and that church grew phenomenally in its stewardship, its ministries, its membership, and its influence in the community. The budget grew from $350,000 to over 1.5 million; a 2.1 million dollar physical facility was built. Ministry that touched all of life was being done, and our mission and ministry funds to the denomination were paid in full! It became a church that lived out the model prayer: "Give us this day, our daily bread!" God provided for whatever was needed to be in ministry!

That experience with Mrs. Ponds became a governing premise of my faith that I have continued to cultivate in my life and ministry. God is faithful and attentive to our needs. The Apostle Paul says in Philippians 4:19, "My God will meet all your needs according to his glorious riches in Christ Jesus" (NIV). There is no doubt about it; God will supply our every need according to his riches in glory!

CENTERED ON GOD'S DEPENDABLE FAITHFULNESS TO US

God never disappoints us and God never lets us down! As I have often heard many of the seasoned saints say in church, "Baby, God will show up and show out!" I can testify to this in my own life. When my mother told me that she could not afford to send me to the college of my choice, faith said I could! When a high school counselor told me I was not college material, faith said I was! When others said I would be making the biggest mistake of my ministerial career by taking a church in Wichita, Kansas, faith said I wouldn't! When some said I was foolish for leaving such a successful ministry in Wichita to go to Dallas to St. Luke, faith said God was with me! God has always made the provisions that were needed to get the job done. I have often heard that where God guides, God will provide.

"Give us this day, our daily bread" is a faith statement. In this ministry, I have had to learn through many experiences, some good and some bad, to trust God in all things. I have had to learn to trust God not just for daily provisions but to take care of the ministry God has entrusted to me. I have had to learn that this is God's thing and not mine. God requires me to walk by faith and not by sight. God will take care of us and calls us to take care of each other.

In teaching and living this aspect of the model prayer, we are growing in the areas of trust, giving, and dependence upon God. No doubt, if we had been in that wilderness for those forty years, we might have tried to gather some extra manna because we would have been somewhat skeptical of a daily miracle. Yet for the children of Israel, living this out became a trust issue, a matter of faith, stuff of the heart!

So often, we struggle with faith because we feel the need to be in charge and in control. Faith challenges us to take our lives, our possessions, our family, our friends, our church, our community, and our world out of our hands and place them in the faithful hands of God.

The Israelites discovered in the wilderness that God was faithful in providing fresh manna daily for the journey. We also need fresh bread for the journey of life every day. We cannot operate or be in ministry of the day-old bread of yesterday, what used to be and what could have been. We need fresh bread for the day's challenges and the ever-changing ministry needs that confront us. "Give us this day our daily bread" so that we will have a fresh outlook on life, openness to God's Spirit, and a bright view of the future God has planned for us. God satisfies the needs of the spirit, the body, the mind, and the world. Our mission is to trust and depend on God to do what God does best—being loving and faithful to us! God can handle our situations! God can handle our churches, our hopes, our dreams, and our ambitions.

All we have to do is put it in the hands of God. We spend most of our time worrying about things we have no control over! We worry about our lives, our survival, our circumstances, our ministries, and our churches. Yet if we stay centered on our commitment to live a prayer-filled life of faith, we can say, "Give us this day our daily bread"! Jesus says in Matthew 6:26, "Look at the birds of the air; they neither sow nor reap nor gather into barns, and yet your heavenly Father feeds them. Are you not of more value than they?"

While on this faith journey I find myself constantly singing:

> Why should I feel discouraged, Why should the
> shadows come,
> Why should my heart be lonely, long for heav'n
> and home;

When Jesus is my portion? My constant Friend is
   He:
His eye is on the sparrow, and I know he watches
   me.
I sing because I'm happy,
I sing because I'm free;
For His eye is on the sparrow,
And I know he watches me. [1]

Lord, teach us to pray, "Give us this day our daily bread!"

QUESTIONS FOR REFLECTION

1. Describe a teachable moment when you learned something. Who was the teacher?

2. Share a time when someone was a blessing to you, a time when you were a blessing to others.

3. Have you ever witnessed a miracle?

4. Where do you need God to sustain you right now?

5. Where in your life do you need to trust and depend on God more?

F.O.C.U.S.—UNITED IN THE POWER AND MINISTRY OF RECONCILIATION

And forgive us our trespasses, as we forgive those who trespass against us. —Matthew 6:12 (Book of Common Prayer)

The call came late one Wednesday night in February of 1989. On the other end of the phone was my mother, in tears, distraught, and saying things I could not believe. She informed me my younger brother, Keith, had been shot and killed in his apartment in Los Angeles. I was in total shock and left numb. How could this be? How could this kind of tragedy hit our family? I mean, we went to church every Sunday! In fact, church is all we knew! We were active in church. As children, my sister, brother, and I had to go whether we wanted to or not. Devastated, I went to the basement of our house in Wichita and sat in the dark in tears the rest of the night. Nothing anyone could say could bring the comfort I really needed. I had lost it emotionally and spiritually.

However, sometime during the next day, while still in a daze, a rage I never felt before entered into the picture. I became angry at the unknown perpetrator of the murder; I became angry at myself for not telling my brother how much I loved and cared for him; and to be honest, I had become angry at God as well! How could God allow my family, my sister, and my mother in particular, go through such a painful and unexplained tragedy?

A few days after this tragedy, the anger toward the perpetrator began to progress into feelings with which I was spiritually and mentally uncomfortable. Ingrained within me were the lessons my mother and so many Sunday school teachers taught me were wrong and certainly unchristian. They went against the fiber of my spiritual being; however, I could not deny them and they were very real. Hatred was taking root in my heart toward the person or persons who snuffed out my brother's life at the tender age of twenty-four, leaving behind two beautiful one-year-old little girls—the same age as my oldest daughter at the time. This tragedy disrupted our entire family circle.

At the funeral service about a week later, I began to rethink, refocus, and allow God's Spirit to work on my heart, mind, and spirit. As our family was preparing to enter the church's sanctuary, looking at the casket at the front of the church containing my brother's body, and with my mother on my arm, I heard Mama begin to mumble words that at first I could not understand. To be honest, I thought Mama, who was taking this loss quite hard, had lost it; and I was trying my best, as the oldest child, to be strong for her and the rest of the family. Yet, as I listened more intently, it was Mama who had it together. It was Mama who really was living and surviving through the awesome power of prayer. I saw her exhibit, even in her grief, everything she had poured into us as children about the power of God that becomes real through prayer. Mother was reciting words of an old gospel hymn, "He Giveth More Grace." In fact, it was a song I was the soloist for with the choir. And it was also one of the songs she requested be sung at the service by the gospel songwriter Margaret Pleasant Douroux and her sister, Norma Pleasant Christmas. I couldn't believe my ears! How could Mama, at a time like this, even talk about grace? In her sorrow, she gave room for it and gave room for praise. From the depths of her hurting heart, she surrendered to prayer! In the midst of her loss, she gave way to forgiveness—even to the perpetrators of this heinous act. Under her breath she kept saying over and over the lyrics of Annie J. Flint, "He giveth more grace, as the burdens grow greater; He sendeth more strength, as the labors increase." [1] What was wrong with mother? She was teaching me that the power of God's grace and love helps move us towards forgiveness and reconciliation.

It was as if a lighting bolt from heaven hit me! It placed me, the preacher of the family, on notice. I began to learn that a prayer-full, focused life, one that lives the Lord's Prayer, is a life that practices forgiveness and moves and participates in a ministry of reconciliation. That was a turning point in my life; I began to see the importance and role the ministry of forgiveness and reconciliation plays out in our lives, ministry, and church. This was not simply an ideal to be touted and proclaimed from pulpits but a life to be lived in the power of the Holy Spirit. How can we truly and honestly be at peace with God and at the same time live at odds with one another? This is exactly the question Jesus helps us answer in the Lord's Prayer.

THE POWER OF LIVING A FORGIVING AND RECONCILING LIFE

In the model prayer, Jesus teaches his disciples and us the power of living a forgiving and reconciling life. He expressed this philosophy at various times and in different ways among his disciples during his ministry. Jesus cuts at the heart of the Mosaic tradition of revenge, retaliation, and retribution. Jesus breaks with long-standing cultural and religious traditions that gave permission to practice an eye for an eye and a tooth for a tooth! Jesus understood the destructive effects of hatred, unresolved conflict, and long-held grudges to the human spirit, and the spiritually devastating repercussions it ultimately has on our relationship with God. Jesus understood the negative toll hatred takes upon us personally, socially, politically, and spiritually. For this time and moment in his ministry, this was a fresh ideal and baffling concept for his disciples; hence the considerable amount of time Jesus spends on the matter with them. It also seems that Jesus must do the same with us as well.

Our witness to this ministry of reconciliation and forgiveness takes place within the backdrop of a world filled with hatred, racism, gender bias, extreme violence, wars, divisions, and phobias of every kind, which are directed against persons who are different from us—culturally, religiously, theologically, racially, socially, and politically. We have seen what hatred, resentment, and grudges have done in our world when it comes to other nations, peoples, religions, and cultures.

We have seen it in race relations in America, in Arab and Jewish conflicts in the Middle East, in radical and fundamental adherence to Christianity and Islam alike. We see it in the violent and unloving way many treat our gay and lesbian sisters and brothers. We see it in the mean-spirited political climate in the American political system. As a pastor and a family member, I have witnessed firsthand what destructive resentment and grudges can do to families, friends, relationships, marriages, ministries, and churches. Families come apart, relationships disintegrate, marriages end, and churches divide because we have not found it in our hearts or beliefs to resolve conflicts, open our hearts to forgiveness, and move toward a ministry of reconciliation. Jesus is clear when he says when you pray say, "Forgive us our trespasses, as we forgive those who trespassed against us."

How Many Times?

It seems Jesus talked about forgiveness and reconciliation so much that Peter asks in Matthew 18:21, "Lord, how many times shall I forgive someone who sins against me? Up to seven times?" (TNIV). Peter seems to think there is a limit to forgiveness—that there is a boundary or a cut-off period! Surely there is a line we can draw in the sand like schoolyard children. "Lord, we can only do this so many times." Yet, Jesus' response surely must have raised eyebrows when he said, "I tell you, not seven times, but seventy-seven times" (TNIV). In other words, as many times as it takes, we are to forgive! As often as God forgives us—we should continue to forgive others. God does not keep count, so we should not keep score; but our lives are steeped in forgiveness and we practice the ministry of reconciliation.

Jesus again must have drawn some gasps from among his teaching crowd when he directly challenges the Mosaic tradition of retribution, retaliation, and revenge in Matthew 5:38-44: "Here's another old saying that deserves a second look: 'Eye for eye, tooth for tooth.' . . . I'm challenging that. I'm telling you to love your enemies. Let them bring out the best in you, not the worst. When someone gives you a hard time, respond with the energies of prayer" (*Message*). Jesus then again says in Luke 6:27-28, "But I say to you that listen, Love your enemies, do good to those who hate you, bless those who curse you, pray for those who abuse you."

I am afraid many Christians look at these sayings as "ideal" statements and goals for which we strive, when in reality they are actual guidelines and rules for kingdom living! We see them as nice moral platitudes but highly impractical in our daily living. How wrong we are! No matter how hard it sounds, Jesus would never ask us to do things that could not be done! In this teachable moment with his disciples and us, Jesus places the challenge before us, saying, as we pray and live, "Forgive us our trespasses as we forgive those who trespass against us."

Martin Luther King, Jr., gave keen insight in his sermon entitled "Loving Your Enemies." My theological understanding of this concept comes from Jesus in the New Testament combined with the study of the life, teachings, and sermons of Dr. Martin Luther King, Jr. Although I was just a child in the sixties, I vividly remember the images from television and witnessed the Watts riots in Los Angeles. I remember the curfew as young African Americans could not be out after dark. I remember seeing the smoke of burning buildings rising in the distance. I remember the television images of water hoses and dogs and the bloodied faces of the "foot soldiers" in the movement for justice and equality. I watched in awe of their nonviolent resistance in the midst of such brutal violence and retribution. Yet, I still hear the eloquent voice of Dr. King's prophetic witness. What's even more dramatic in Dr. King's teaching of nonviolence is his embrace of Jesus' understanding of this thing called "love." Dr. King says:

> I am certain that Jesus understood the difficulty inherent in the act of loving one's enemy. He never joined the ranks of those who talk glibly about the easiness of the moral life. He realized that every genuine expression of love grows out of a consistent and total surrender to God. So when Jesus said, "Love your enemy," he was not unmindful of the stringent

qualities. Yet he meant every word of it. Our responsibility as Christians is to discover the meaning of this command and seek passionately to live it out in our daily lives. [2]

Jesus is definitely calling us to a ministry of forgiveness and reconciliation!

We were created to be in relationships. We were created to be in relationship with God and our fellow human beings. However, sin has done severe damage to our relationships with both God and others. The Apostle Paul says in 2 Corinthians 5:20, "So we are ambassadors for Christ, since God is making his appeal through us; we entreat you on behalf of Christ, be reconciled to God." When distrust surfaces, hurts are experienced, wounds inflicted, and ties broken—once-intimate relationships are severely damaged. For reconciliation to be experienced, we must see forgiveness as the first step toward the repair of what has been broken. Howard Thurman, in his book *Jesus and the Disinherited*, eloquently points out that in order for forgiveness and reconciliation to take place, there must be the acknowledgement that a wrong has been done and an open desire to repair the damaged relationship must be experienced. He says that "reconciliation is the will to reestablish a relationship. It involves confession of error and a seeking to be restored to one's former place." [3]

WHY FORGIVE AT ALL?

We forgive because we have been forgiven by God. We forgive because our broken relationship with God has been reestablished. We forgive because we have been restored. God refuses to hang our errors, faults, and sins over our heads; therefore, we are called to live in the same way toward others. We are a part of God's ministry of reconciliation because we have been reconciled to God. Our relationship has been restored and our fellowship with the divine reestablished. From that experience we are now empowered to do the same toward others from whom we too have been estranged! Through Christ, relationships are restored, community reestablished, and barriers broken because God was in Christ and reconciled the world unto God's self. In other words, we work toward reconciliation with one another because of our reestablished relationship with God. Our relationship with God ultimately affects our relationships with each other. A prayer-filled, focused life is one whose aim and goal is to be reconciled with others and to work toward reconciliation in all areas of human life and existence.

In this teachable moment with his disciples, Jesus said when we pray we should say, "Forgive us our trespasses, as we forgive those who trespass against us." Of course, this is the traditional rendition of the Lord's Prayer. Some other translations use the term "debts" and "debtors" instead of "trespasses" and "trespass." For the benefit of our discussion, I prefer the term "trespass" over "debts." Debts and debtors carry the connotation of something being owed to someone. However, "trespass" denotes the fact that someone has caused injury or hurt and implies that someone has intruded upon another's dignity. "Trespass" points to the breaking of a moral or social code. This, for me, is a much stronger term than "debts." We have trespassed against God, caused injury to God's creation, trampled God's code of conduct, and have broken God's moral and social law. We have also trespassed against others and others have trespassed against us. We have at times done things unknowingly or knowingly against our brothers and sisters, which has indeed intruded upon their dignity as one created in the image of God. We have harbored ill feelings for those who have wronged us, breathing the air of revenge and retribution instead of learning to let it go!

LET GO OF THE HURTS

Living the Lord's Prayer is a call for us to let go of the hurts, release the grudges, and settle and bring closure to the grievances we have toward those who may have brought pain into our lives. It is that bitterness that we harbor in our minds and hearts that defiles the human spirit and fractures human relationships. It gnaws and pulls at us, chipping away at us spiritually, mentally, emotionally, and physically. It may have been done personally or corporately, individually or institutionally; it might be social or political. It must be released! We will never fully be the persons God created us to be with this anguish pulling at our souls. Forgiveness is the path that leads toward release of the poison of bitterness of a hurt, a wrong, an unkind word, or an activity that first brought anguish to one's spirit.

Of course, when we are wronged, hurt, or mistreated, the typical immediate feelings that surface within us are the old triplets: retribution, revenge, and retaliation. We want to get even! We want to be judge, jury, and executioner; in fact, we want to play God! We quickly latch on to the Mosaic code of justice: an eye for an eye; and a tooth for a tooth. In the Lord's Prayer, Jesus lays out a model his disciples are expected to live by. We don't operate by the culture's standards but by the kingdom standards! We don't operate from the arena of retribution, revenge, or retaliation, but out of an understanding of forgiveness. For many Christians, it might be stated how unrealistic and challenging this is to carry out; however, I firmly again declare that the Lord would never ask us to do anything we cannot be empowered to do through the gift of the Holy Spirit! Again, it must be reiterated that this is not simply an idealistic concept, but a lifestyle to be lived.

I have often heard, "I cannot forgive because I cannot forget!" It must be understood that Jesus' concept of forgiveness is not forgetting per se. It is not sweeping the incident or conduct under the rug. Forgiveness in no way condones either the conduct or the perpetrated wrong; neither does it mean we become a doormat to be mistreated and disrespected by others or society. Forgiveness is not even the absence or the abdication of justice. Rather, forgiveness is the extension of one's hand in reconciliation! It is the bringing together of those who were once at odds, holding one another in mutual respect and reverence for who we are as children of God. We saw this in action as Jesus was crucified. Hanging on a cross, looking at his accusers, executioners, followers who abandoned him and a thief who mocked him, he said, "Father, forgive them for they know not what they do." He extended the hand of reconciliation, and refused to allow their actions to change how they should be seen as children of God who deserved the respect and reverence and were treated as such.

While attending the World Methodist Conference in Seoul, Korea, in July of 2006, I heard Dr. Evelyn Parker, Professor at Perkins School of Theology at Southern Methodist University in Dallas say, "By his actions, Jesus teaches us that forgiveness frees us from the chains of revenge and moves toward a ministry of reconciliation." In that vein, Dr. King says, "It is also necessary to realize that the forgiving act must always be initiated by the person who has been wronged."[4] That is what happened on the cross and that is what should take place through us as those who live by the principles of the Lord's Prayer. It does not mean justice will not be served, but rather it means we no longer live with revenge and retribution in our hearts. Let me reiterate, forgiveness is not the absence of justice. We can still forgive without preventing God's justice from being carried out.

UNITED IN FORGIVENESS AND RECONCILIATION

Forgiveness in action was recently seen as the country was shocked and horrified by the tragic shooting of Amish school children in Pennsylvania. The story broke our hearts and caused us to wonder what kind of deranged person could perpetrate such a despicable act. The Amish showed this nation what the kingdom is really like! They took us to task and gave us a practical course in Christian Discipleship 101! They taught us how true Christian forgiveness ought to look. Many of us in our Christian nation thought their actions were strange and abnormal. Were they? I think not! They were normative for practicing disciples of Jesus Christ. I saw the face and felt the spirit of Christ as I followed the story. They expressed divine love for the family of the perpetrator of this heinous act. They forgave them and they forgave him! The world wondered how they could do so. They should demand justice be served right then and there!

The Amish reactions were not a sign of weakness but a demonstration of great divine strength! They were a witness to the world, more so than those of us who consider ourselves a part of so-called mainstream Christianity. As we enjoy and embrace all that modern technology has to offer, can we practice forgiveness as they do? The Amish were practitioners of what we preach! They lived the model prayer while we so often just pray it! I am reminded of something I read in the newspaper concerning this. The quote comes from an unnamed Amish woman when asked how they could forgive when this horrible tragedy shocked their tiny community to its core. She says, "We have to forgive. We have to forgive him (the murderer) in order for God to forgive us." What powerful words! Jesus said, "When you pray say... Forgive us our trespasses as we forgive those who trespass against us." It took such a horrible act to show us what forgiveness looks like.

Neither that tiny community nor the world will or can forget the abominable act, but we can forgive the perpetrator of it! Forgiveness is not forgetting. It is a move toward reconciliation in relationships that have been fractured by sin and offensive actions. It is putting into practice a love that loves persons unconditionally. As Martin Luther King, Jr., taught us, it is loving one's enemies in such a way that does not allow the wrongs done to us to keep us from seeing and treating others as they really are, children of God, created in God's image! He says, "Forgiveness does not mean ignoring what has been done or putting a false label on an evil act. It means, rather, that the evil act no longer remains as a barrier to the relationship." [5] He goes on to say, "But when we forgive, we forget in the sense that the evil deed is no longer a mental block impeding a new relationship." [6] The measure we are able to forgive is indicative of the measure we are able to love.

The model prayer unites us as we participate in the power of the ministry of reconciliation. We have been blessed to be a forgiven people; therefore, we live life with a forgiving spirit. Our forgiveness by God cannot be understood if we don't practice forgiveness toward others. Being unforgiving and a harborer of resentment are in conflict with the lifestyle of the forgiven. It is at odds with the love God has poured out on us. According to Jesus' teachings, being unforgiving is tantamount to living an *unfocused* life rather that one that is focused on the goals and standards of the kingdom. It is a contradiction! God offers forgiveness to us unconditionally and expects us to offer forgiveness to others as a witness to the world that God's love is stronger than hate.

Every day, as we witness acts of injustice, racism, sexism, corporate greed, and political indifference to the plight of the have-nots in the world, we must continue to allow the Holy Spirit to work with our hearts and minds and keep our focus on the standards and goals of the kingdom. When we are wronged and offended by the actions of others, we must be empowered to live this prayer! It becomes difficult at times, but with God all things are possible and we can do all things through Christ who will give us the strength! I find myself struggling with it every day. Right when I feel I've finally got it, tomorrow I'll read about another tragedy, see another act of injustice, or even personally experience another offense, and maybe mistreat another, and it might be another story. We then must once again turn to the God who is loving, merciful, and forgiving, who will then remind us that as a forgiven people we are to live forgiving lives that work toward a ministry of reconciliation! Ephesians 4:32 reminds us: "Be gentle with one another, sensitive. Forgive one another as quickly and thoroughly as God in Christ forgave you" (*Message*). We are called as disciples to live forgiving lives that lead to building bridges to repair breaches. As citizens of the kingdom, we are united in a ministry of reconciliation! What God has done for us in Christ Jesus, we walk together to live that with one another! Lord, please teach us how to pray!

QUESTIONS FOR REFLECTION

1. Share a time when you were forgiven.

2. Share a time when you needed forgiveness.

3. How would your life be different if people stood together to forgive and offer reconciliation?

4. How does your church encourage forgiveness and reconciliation? Can you think of a time when the church, as a body of believers, offered forgiveness?

5. Is there an area or a relationship in your own life that needs God's healing touch today?

CHAPTER 6

F.O.C.U.S.—Strong
and Solid in the
Struggle

*And do not bring us to the time of trial, but rescue us
from the evil one. —Matthew 6:13*

We all remember where we were and what we were doing on that infamous Tuesday morning of September 11, 2001. I was in Los Angeles attending a denominational committee meeting of Strengthening the Black Church for the 21st Century, where I had been since that past Sunday night. On that Tuesday morning, I had been scheduled to bring the morning devotion. I got up early, around five o'clock, to review and prepare for the message of the day. The room was quiet, television off, and the terror gripping the country and the shock rumbling through the world had not yet reached me.

In the midst of studying the outline and reviewing the scripture, my wife, Marsha, called me. Sounding frantic, she said, "Turn on the T.V.!" My response was, "For what?" She simply said, "Something is happening, you just need to turn on the television!" When I turned it on, my eyes, like everyone else's in the country, were fixated on a news show. For me it was the *Today Show*, and Katie Couric was reporting that a plane had flown into the World Trade Center in New York. My first thought was this was an accident involving a small private plane. Little did I know at that moment that the world as we knew it was about to change! This was not an accident with a small plane but an attack using passenger planes as missiles with innocent and helpless victims onboard.

None of us could believe what was unfolding before us that day. While watching the report, none of us could believe our eyes as we saw another figure that looked like a plane slam into the second tower. It was becoming increasingly clear that this was not an accident but a deliberate planned attack on American soil. The devotion I was preparing was placed on the corner of the desk in my room. What I was planning to say was no longer relevant. In fact, I don't even remember what it was, but I do remember as if it were yesterday what I did say! It was, "What do you do when all hell breaks loose?" I later expanded those words to be that Sunday's sermon at Saint Mark Church in Wichita. As the morning progressed, we heard of the other jetliners, which crashed into the Pentagon and in a field in Pennsylvania.

We all were numb as we watched the towers crumble with all of those lives trapped inside. We were informed all air traffic had been halted. Being at an airport hotel in my hometown of Los Angeles, I could actually see the runways and terminals at Los Angeles International Airport out the windows of my room. I had never seen the airport in such disarray. Planes were only landing and none were taking off. Eventually all traffic halted. It was eerie seeing LAX so quiet with no activity as air traffic in the whole country came to a screeching halt.

Our committee was stranded together in Los Angeles, not knowing when or how we would get back home. On top of that, the chairperson of our committee, Bishop Jonathan Keaton had done something that pierced my very being. He went to the hotel management and informed them that a bunch of United Methodists pastors were there in a meeting and we would gladly assist and minister to the affected families as needed. You see, originally, we were told that the hotel in which we were staying was to be the gathering place for the families of one of the doomed flights. *How could he do this to us?* I thought. *What would we say? More specifically, what would I say? How could we provide the needed words to families who were in such shock?* I thought, *Bishop! I don't have the foggiest idea of what to say or do at a time like this!* Seminary did not prepare or train me for such a horrific tragedy! What words of comfort could I give those families or even to a congregation back home during this time of national grief, anger, and mourning?

September 11 forced me do some deep soul-searching and intense theological reflection. How could anyone deliberately do anything so despicable, contemptible, and abominable with and to innocent lives? What could possess anyone to have such hatred they would be willing to carry out such an evil act in the name of God? This caused me to take another look at the face of evil and temptation that is present in the world. It brought evil up close. Evil and temptation are corporate and personal. They can cause us all, on a given day, with certain circumstances at points in our lives, to have the capacity to do things that cause pain, hurt, destruction, and injury to others. Jesus knew evil's power to lure, entice, infect, and affect us all! Jesus knew the impact it could have on our choices and decisions. He knew its devastating power in the world, in our lives and communities; therefore, he teaches us to live and leave our mark in life by living a focused life saying, "And do not bring us to the time of trial, but rescue us from the evil one."

There are absolutes in life and in the world that we all must face. That is one of the lessons of this tragedy we all endured. It brought some beliefs forth I knew to be true but had pushed to the back burner. There was the tendency in the church to only deal and talk about God's goodness, God's grace, God's mercy, and God's forgiveness because there are many theological concepts we mainline denominations don't like to talk about. There are terms and identifications we do not like using. We don't like talking about and are uncomfortable with terms like sin, evil, Satan, and the Evil One. We feel there is a danger in wrapping evil and its impact on the world into a single personality. However, we need to bring some things back into theological focus!

September 11 helped to solidify and drive the point home that if there is good, then there has to be evil! If there is right, then there is wrong. If there is righteousness, then there is unrighteousness. If there is salvation, then there is sin. Here's the one that might cause some to shake their heads, but is so true for me; if there is God, then there is Satan! Satan is not equal to God, but that does not diminish Satan's reality. In other words, there is a power at war with God's plan, God's will, and God's direction for this world and our lives! Just because we don't like to talk about Satan, the Evil One, or the devil, does not dismiss the reality of demonic activity in the world! Whether we choose to believe it or not, there is a diabolical power at work trying to uproot and destroy the seeds of God's kingdom that have been planted in the hearts and minds of human beings. Yet, it is the focused, prayer-filled life that battles the Evil One with the strength the Lord provides to go head-to-head with evil's influence and destructive nature. As Dr. Martin Luther King, Jr., said in the eulogy of the young black girls killed in the bombing of a Birmingham Church in 1963, "God still has a way of wringing good out of evil." [1]

THE CHOICES WE MAKE

Temptation, sin, and evil go a little deeper than what was drilled into my psyche those early years as a youth in church. It seems to me that back then, temptation, sin, and evil were limited to drinking, smoking, partying, sex (premarital and adultery), gambling, and yes, even playing cards. I never will forget being called on the carpet with several other college students who were home for the summer before the General Assembly of the Sunday school to publicly apologize for playing the card game "Spades" at the church picnic! Can you imagine that? I could not believe what was happening, and I was really getting hot under the collar for being called out and placed on the spot like that. Why in the world were we being singled out for playing an innocent game of cards when a bunch of deacons were under a tree playing Dominoes? What was the difference? We were not gambling or anything, just some young people having fun at a church function! This limited and narrow definition of sin keeps us from being on the forefront of the struggle to ensure that all of God's children have access to the abundant life that Jesus wants to provide in the midst of evil's underhanded tactics to kill, steal, and destroy all of life!

Such narrow and erroneous definitions of temptations, sin, and evil keep us isolated from the wider effects of their devastation that we are seeing unleashed in the world. For Jesus, temptation and evil are the main antagonists in the battle for the kingdom and can block us from ushering in the kingdom of God. The concepts of temptation and evil must be seen in terms that are deeper than simply our personal moral failings, but must include our corporate failings to the standards of God's rule of law, purpose, and will for all of humanity and this created world. Temptation and evil not only destroy us personally, but corporately as well when we violate God's creation and disregard the humanity of other human beings created in the very image of God. We do the message and power of the gospel a huge disservice when we place all our emphasis on personal temptation and evil and ignore the wider devastation of corporate and social temptation and evil that affect whole groups of peoples and nations!

We are struggling with the temptation of evil when we look the other way from the thousands upon thousands who sleep under freeway underpasses. We cannot sit idly by and do nothing when we see the vicious cycle of poverty being perpetuated by political decisions that disfigure the image of God in the least of these! That is evil! We cannot ignore the fact that millions have no health care or limited access to it! That is evil! We cannot turn a blind eye to the plight of abused children and women who are fighting for their very survival! That is evil! The prayer-full, focused life is one that has been empowered to fight temptation and the evil it births when we act and respond to it! Jesus says, when you pray—or as I like to put it, as you live—say, "And do not bring us to the time of trial, but rescue us from the evil one."

We all face choices in life. Every day we stand at the crossroads and must choose the way we will travel and live this day. Daily, the choices between good and evil, justice and injustice, right and wrong, righteousness and unrighteousness, are before us. They are a part of life that shapes and sharpens us as committed disciples of Jesus Christ. Our choices will speak life or death; bring peace or destruction;

and result in joy or pain. That is the reason Jesus teaches us to pray, "And do not bring us to the time of trial, but rescue us from the evil one."

This teachable moment with Jesus and his disciples helps us understand what is needed to handle evil in the world and in our lives, and also to overcome the temptations we will face to either do good or evil. Jesus points us in the right direction in handling evil and temptation. Our power, in this struggle, comes from our relationship with him. He directs us to seek God's power to stay focused and strong as we disentangle the ravages of evil in this world and the temptations that can either make or break us as disciples of Jesus Christ. We don't just pray this prayer but we live it with the power of the Holy Spirit, which guides us in our decision-making process with the choices we all must make.

EVIL IS ALWAYS PRESENT

We don't have to look far to see the ramifications of wrong choices when faced with temptation and the effects of evil in the world. Living a focused life is a call to make the right choices in combating the devastation and influence evil can bring in our lives, our relationships, society, and world. According to our biblical tradition in Genesis, evil has been around since the beginning of time, ever since the first man and woman appeared on the scene and had to choose between death and life. Wrong choices distort the image in which we have been created; and yielding to evil attacks us from the very being of our hearts and affects our actions, individually and collectively.

Historically, socially, and individually, we see evil's fingerprints and handiwork in the world. We saw it in the slave trade, the Holocaust, the Spanish Inquisition, the apartheid system of South Africa, Jim Crow, segregation, and discriminatory practices in America; we saw it in the ethnic cleansing in Bosnia, the chaos of the Middle East; we saw it in the attacks of September 11, the bombings in London subways; we see it in the neglect of the world powers in the fight against the AIDS pandemic in sub-Saharan Africa. We see it in racism and sexism even today. Evil is busy bringing destruction, death, and disruption through human design and actions, and even worse, through our inaction. Evil grows powerful by our silence in the face of demonic schemes. Living the Lord's Prayer is a call for us to speak out and confront evil's diabolical plans and plots! Evil's influence and power is at work in the world; and Jesus teaches us that a focused life is lived through praying "and do not bring us to a time of trial, but rescue us from the evil one."

We are asking God to guard us from being imprisoned and influenced by destructive passions, feelings, and inactions that can bring harm to ourselves, to others, and to the world. We are asking the Lord to help us model right choices that will bring the best out of us and not act out the worst in us! We know all too well that the potential to do either is there. We struggle with two natures, according to our Christian theology. The Apostle Paul would say we are struggling with two natures, one good and one evil; one being influenced by God and the other being influenced by the Evil One. The choices we make will determine which nature will come out on top!

Our lives are lived and influenced in light of our choices. However, making those choices may not be as easy as it might appear on the surface. It is a struggle! As human beings we are pulled in various directions. We are dependent upon God, as we live focused lives, to keep us open and discerning of God's Spirit so that we can choose what is right and good for the kingdom and our lives. As we live the Lord's Prayer, we are seeking God's guidance in all of life so that we make the right choices that bring glory to God, build the kingdom, and give witness to God's love. Daily before us are decisions and choices that bring life or destruction.

JESUS KNOWS ALL ABOUT OUR STRUGGLES

Every day our struggle as human beings is to just do the right thing! We are clear that we are empowered to make the right choices that will bring glory to God, enhance our witness as Christ's disciples, and participate in the church's mission to make disciples for Jesus Christ for the transformation of the world. At the end of each day, we have to recall things said, deeds done, and things left undone. We must realize we often come up short! Staying strong in this struggle to do the right things is part of the journey of our discipleship. Jesus knew the struggles we would face as his disciples, so in the model prayer he teaches us to pray, "And do not bring us to the time of trial, but rescue us from the evil one." Jesus was well aware of what we would be facing and what his disciples would be encountering. I can remember, when I was growing up, the amens spoken through the church as we would sing:

> Jesus knows all about our struggles, He will guide till the day is done; There's not a friend like the lowly Jesus—No, not one! No, not one! [2]

These choices are ever before us, but so is God! The Lord is there to help and guide us in making the right ones as we are discerning of God's will. These choices will enhance life or uproot lives, bring joy or cause pain, give hope or bring despair. Our choices will either fulfill our lives or leave them empty with regrets. This is the very issue underlining Jesus' teaching of the model prayer. He is not simply teaching us how to pray; more important, he is teaching us how to live making the right choices. A focused, prayer-full life is open and attuned to God's beckoning and prodding, so we struggle with making the right life choices for the betterment and equality of all humanity.

Jesus teaches us that we have, with God's help, the power and strength to overcome temptation and combat the evil in the world and in our lives. "And do not bring us to the time of trial, but rescue us from the evil one." This is a deep statement of faith that begs our theological reflection! It challenges us to think through our beliefs, theology, and views on the problem of evil, the meaning of good, what temptation is, and the role God plays in it all.

Most of us have grown up reciting this section of the Lord's Prayer as such, "And lead us not into temptation, but deliver us from evil." Whichever way we pray it, there is ever before us the constant reminder of the reality of temptation and evil we face daily in our lives.

At face value, it appears we are praying as if it is the Lord who guides us into the path of temptation and evil's harm and destruction. We are clear that this is not the case. Temptation does not come from God and evil is not God's doing! God does not tempt us to do evil and God does not bring evil upon us! That is contrary to the very nature of God! However, by living a focused, prayer-full life, we will be confronted with choices and decisions that can build the kingdom with good or dishonor the kingdom with evil! We are a part of the cosmic struggle between good and evil, God and Satan, righteousness and unrighteousness.

We are in the midst of a spiritual battle! It is a battle for the souls, minds, hearts, and lives of our nation, our communities, our churches, and one another. We are broken and fallen as human beings who struggle daily with becoming who God creates us to be. Ephesians 6:10-12 is a vivid portrayal of what the focused life must endure on a regular basis:

> Finally, be strong in the Lord and in the strength of his power. Put on the whole armor of God, so that you may be able to stand against the wiles of the devil. For our struggle is not against enemies of blood and flesh, but against the rulers, against the authorities, against the cosmic powers of this present darkness, against the spiritual forces of evil in the heavenly places.

We live with choices. Choices with ramifications that not only affect ourselves but also those around us, the environment, and the world order! We must choose and discern between what is good, right, and just and what is evil. We must choose between what is from heaven or from the pits of hell; what is right or what is wrong; what is of God or the Evil One. The bottom line and the rule of thumb of our choices and decisions over temptation and evil is this: does it hinder or enhance life? Does it restore relationships or drive a wedge between others? Does it build community or destroy and uproot them? Will our choices help others or injure them? Does the choice encourage and empower others to live out their potential or does it stifle, suppress, or oppress? That is the difference between doing good and doing evil! It is all about our choice's effect upon the lives and living conditions of all of God's children!

This discussion and reflection brought to mind a sermon I preached a few years ago entitled "Tell the Devil to Shut Up!" In that word, the challenge was for us to confront evil by silencing its voice, influence, and power in our lives, in our society, and world. Whatever evil and temptation have spoken into the lives of others, society, and communities and hold them hostage to defeat, oppression, and despair, we are called to work to silence its influence and power through our decisions, choices, and strategies of liberation, wholeness, healing, and deliverance. A focused, prayer-filled life operates from a position of spiritual power and not spiritual weakness.

The Lord's word of peace can diffuse evil's words and actions of war! The Lord's word of love can overcome evil's words and actions of hate! The Lord's word of tolerance and acceptance can undercut evil's words and actions of exclusion and prejudice! The Lord's word of hope and light can shatter evil's word of depression and darkness! The Lord's word of grace can destroy evil's word of self-hate and low self-esteem! The Lord's word of salvation can uproot evil's word of condemnation! The Lord's word of liberation can conquer evil's word of bondage and slavery! A focused life will confront and fight evil's demonic actions in our lives, our world, and communities. We can do it!

Evil has spoken loudly in our nation, world, and communities. It can cause us to lose hope! Dr. Frank A. Thomas, the senior pastor of Mississippi Boulevard Christian Church in Memphis, Tennessee, writes: "Jesus understood the true power, nature, size, scope, depth, reality, and impact of evil. Jesus understood that evil is so despicable, so desperate, so depraved, so destructive, so vicious, and so able to bring death, misery, and pain"[3] that Jesus gave us authority to deal with it and confront it face-to-face!

It is for this reason that St. Luke "Community" is heavily involved in outreach and social action in the community. God calls us to be spiritual foot soldiers to guard and work against the influence and the works of evil in our society. St. Luke "Community" sees as its mission and vision to be a proclaimer of the gospel of Jesus Christ through the prophetic voice of liberation and transformation, so persons can reach their full potential and become all God has created us to become. Our outreach and social action ministry witness runs the gamut from ministry to those infected and affected by HIV/AIDS to speaking and rallying against the genocide in the Darfur region of Sudan or the racial injustices being practiced in places like Jena, Louisiana! On any given day, you will see and experience members and ministries of St. Luke combating the evils that plague so many lives and communities locally and globally.

St. Luke is not afraid to make its voice heard and presence felt in every arena of society where evil has raised its demonic head. In the school systems, issues of homelessness and hunger, drug and alcohol addictions, political and social issues that affect *the least of these* will be arenas in which you will find the church at work! St. Luke's ministry is felt as far away as Zimbabwe, in orphanages where children have lost parents to the pandemic of AIDS, and at Africa University, to ensure young people on the continent have access to a college education, and as close to the community where we reside as relief to Hurricane Katrina and Rita evacuees, school supplies, ensuring all young people have an equal chance for success, immunizations for those who can least afford it, and to be the community gathering place where residents can discuss and mobilize for actions. This is living the Lord's Prayer in a focused way of Christian discipleship. We do it knowing that our faith and work is not in vain.

I am reminded of a scene in the comedy movie *Sister Act* when the Mother Superior, played by Maggie Smith, is so adamantly opposed to the nuns moving out of the convent into the community, which was being advocated by Whoopi Goldberg's character, Sister Mary Clarence. Sister Mary Clarence is pushing hard to get the nuns out of their self-imposed prison behind the church's walls and into the community to touch the lives of those around it. In the middle of the big blowout between Sister Mary Clarence and Mother Superior, Sister Mary Patrick, played by Kathy Najimy, that it is time for them to get out and help in the community! Sister Mary Patrick says, "There is so much we can do to help besides just pray!"

How true! There is so much we can do as the body of Christ to bring and effect change, transformation, and liberation in the world by living as focused, prayerful disciples who model life after the teachings of the Lord's Prayer! Yes, we can pray but when we are done praying, it is time to roll up our sleeves and get to work! Jesus is counting on us! The Holy Spirit is waiting to work with us! And God will empower us! The temptation to overlook or ignore the needs of others is the Evil One's greatest weapon used against those of us who call ourselves Christian. Living the Lord's Prayer causes us to be spiritually attuned and aware of those inner workings within us that tempt us to do what is contrary to the will, purpose, and movement of God in the world. That spiritual intuition gives us the power to resist the promptings of the Evil One in our lives, choices, and decisions.

Temptation and evil are real and must be faced head on. As I learned through an old gospel Sunday school hymn, temptation is not the sin because it is experienced by all of us. It is succumbing to its lure and yielding to its influence that unleashes evil, destruction, and hurt in the world. Remember that old song? "Yield not to temptation, For yielding is sin; Each vict'ry will help you Some other to win; Fight valiantly onward, Dark passions subdue; Look ever to Jesus, He'll carry you through. Ask the Savior to help you, Comfort, strengthen, and keep you; He is willing to aid you, He will carry you through."[4]

We can do battle against the ravages of temptation and evil! It is not out of our reach; but to the contrary, the power to overcome is already at work in our hearts. Victory is already ours, for the power of the Lord is already at work in us, which helps us overcome temptation and to win the struggle against evil's influence in the world. The writer of 1 John 4:4 speaks an encouraging word in the midst of our daily struggles against sin, evil, and temptation. That passage says, "For the one who is in you is greater than the one who is in the world." Jesus' challenge gives us the much-needed hope we must have to live a focused, prayer-full life because it reminds us that with God's help and power, temptation and evil will not have the last word! By our living and example we pray, "And do not bring us to the time of trial, but rescue us from the evil one." Lord, please teach us how to pray!

QUESTIONS FOR REFLECTION

1. Who has made a difference in your life?

2. If you had the power to right one wrong, what would it be?

3. Where do you need to stay strong right now in your faith? Where does your church need to stay strong?

4. How do you care for the least of these? What kinds of ministry do you believe God is calling you or your church to do?

5. What are you doing to fight the temptations you face?

CHAPTER 7

LIVING THE DOXOLOGY

For thine is the kingdom, and the power, and the glory,
for ever. Amen. —Matthew 6:13 (KJV)

M ost ancient manuscripts of the Gospel of Matthew do not contain the doxology of the Lord's Prayer. In most translations, it is a postscript, including the New Revised Standard Version. For its inclusion, we have turned to the classic King James Version's translation of the prayer. I felt compelled to include it because this is the way most of us learned it and continue to pray and sing it. Also, the ancient church thought it an important addition to be used as the prayer's doxology, so that the prayer fittingly ends with this expression of praise and glorifying God. After all is said and done, we are to place all things in God's hands, "For thine is the kingdom, and the power and the glory, for ever."

A doxology points to the One in whom we live, we move, and we have our being. It is a designated conclusion that states that life and its ultimate fulfillment is in the hands of God. God is in control of life. In fact, as African American slaves would sing, "God's got the whole world in [God's] hands!" In my humble opinion, no prayer is complete without a doxology. No prayer is complete without glorifying God, the One who sustains, upholds, and guides us in all truth. So it stands to reason that no focused prayer-full life would be complete without a living doxology; which is a life that breathes and lives out its expression of praise and glory to God by the standards of this that we call the Lord's Prayer.

The traditional setting of this prayer begins with God and ends with God and all throughout it is focused on God! A focused, prayer-filled life, patterned after the Lord's Prayer, points to God, depends on God, and looks to God for its fulfillment. Everything in it, around it, and in between it is designed to glorify God and build up the kingdom of God. Our lives are a doxology because we know the ultimate reality is that this is God's thing, God's doing, and ultimately, *God is in control* for its fulfillment! The doxology of the Lord's Prayer is crucial, as it points to the power that undergirds our striving and reaching for the goals of the kingdom because it tells us whose kingdom this really is and its driving power of guidance and rule.

We have maintained the premise throughout our discussion that the Lord's Prayer is not so much designed to be a prayer spoken as it is a prayer to be lived. This is not a call to prayer as we know it, with bowed heads and folded hands, but is Jesus' clarion call for us to live for God's glory by being the standard bearers of the kingdom's standards! This is a call to live the abundant life, which cannot be accomplished or experienced apart from God's power and strength.

The doxology becomes our statement of faith and reminds us that God will accomplish what God has set in motion. Nothing can prevent God from doing what God has set out to do! Evil's demonic tactics may stifle the kingdom's goals, but it will not ultimately be victorious over them. Therefore, a doxology is appropriate. It is God's kingdom that is advancing forward! God is the power that helps us live by the kingdom's goals, operate by its standards, and walk in its way. The praise for all that has been done, is being done, and will be done in the name of the Lord's kingdom belongs solely to God!

GOD'S PURPOSE FOR OUR LIVES

Our purpose in life is to live for God's glory and give the world a glimpse of what the kingdom of God is like. This focused, prayer-filled lifestyle, outlined in the Lord's Prayer, is but a shadowy glimpse of how we humans can show the world how we are to live in relation to God, the world, material things, and each other. It points to a life rooted and dependent upon God for all that is needed to live the focused, abundant, prayer-filled life. This life does not merely depend on God for some things; it depends on God for *all* things! No prayer is designed to tell God what we need and use God as a cosmic bellhop, spiritual Santa Claus, or a divine ATM machine, but spirit-lived and breathed prayer is the acknowledgement of our ultimate need for God!

Sometimes in ministry, especially in what we like to call "successful" ministry, we start to think we can do it all. In some instances, we delude ourselves into thinking this is our doing. That is one of the temptations with which we struggle in the ministry. A focused life constantly reminds us this is God's doing! What will be done or accomplished will take place only through the help of the Lord. For me, it is a reminder we are a part of the ultimate plans and will of God, and our lifestyle of prayer is petitioning God to allow us to be a part of what God is doing.

Once, in a meeting with pastors, Bishop Dick Wills, at the time serving as the senior pastor of Christ Church in Ft.

Lauderdale, said something that was thought-provoking and spiritually enlightening. His comments radically changed my prayer life and how I would seek God's direction. Bishop Wills chastised us for always praying and asking God "to bless us in what we are doing!" That is what we tend to do! We want God to bless this and bless that. It is as if we have already made the plans and planned the party and then want God to pay for it! Instead, he challenged us to ask God to take us or better yet, allow us to participate in what God was already blessing. We do not need God to sanction our work; we need to be a part of God's work. This is God's work! This is God's plan! This is God's way! And it should be our desire to be a part of what God is already doing. It is not our agenda but God's. That is why it is "your kingdom come; your will be done," and not our kingdom or our will! We must be clear in our actions if this is what we want done—or *is* this what God wants done?

A focused, prayer-filled life is not a sign of weakness but points to a true sense of self and strength. As the doxology of the Lord's Prayer teaches us that the thing for which we are reaching is ultimately God's thing, a focused life is clear that everything we do and accomplish is because of God. We are not self-employed when it comes to God's kingdom—we are God-employed! What we do still is dependent upon God.

That is what keeps me going in ministry. If this were dependent upon me, I would have thrown in the towel a long time ago. I am clear that this is God's doing and God will assume full responsibility in fulfilling God's will and purpose for life, society, the church, and the ministry. The focused life is one that has a desire to participate in what God is already doing in the world. That is why everything we do for the kingdom begins with God, is empowered by God, and ends with God.

IN THE MEANTIME

The focused, prayer-filled life is a life of hope and faith. It is one that is constantly reminded that no matter how bad things are, this is not the end of the story. God will have the final word when it all is said and done. Our hope and faith tell us that the ultimate fulfillment of the kingdom of God lies in the future. Yet, we are called to live in the present or what I like to call, *"in the meantime."* Although we know that this is a future reality, God has called us to live by the standards of the Lord's Prayer, as it helps us be the visible representatives and human signs of what the kingdom is like and of greater things to come. New Testament theologian Douglas Hare says, "We cannot build the kingdom of God on Earth, because even our best efforts toward peace, justice, and community are compromised by sin. Only God can bring the ultimate transformation that includes the radical annulment of sin." [1] Yet we are called to live in it and work toward it. That is why the doxology is such a big part of who we are as focused, prayer-full, hope-filled, and faith-walking ambassadors of the kingdom. Faith says God will bring it to pass. "Final mending of the fission which exists between God and humankind is the ultimate end of Christian strivings." [2] Knowing this does not hinder our kingdom call; rather it informs, focuses, and enhances it. This helps us live the doxology.

I wasn't very good in sports, except for swimming. You get me in water back in the day, I could give you a run for your money. But when it came to baseball, basketball, or touch football, you might as well forget it. I would rather watch it than play it because I was so insecure in my abilities. In elementary school, when the captains of the teams would choose their players, it was disheartening and bruising to the ego to see them go down the line choosing person after person until they got down to the worst ones, which included me. I was always one of the last chosen.

On the field or on the court, I tried to do my part, but I did not have the skills or abilities of the other boys on the team. I tried my best to make some kind of contribution, no matter how small or humble. But when the team won, I still felt a part of the win! I might have been one of the last chosen, but I was still part of the winning team!

That is how it is with God's work and God's kingdom; we don't have everything it takes or even the best skills, and sometimes we don't even have the best of intentions; however, we contribute our part and we know that in the end we are on the winning team! We do what we do because we know we are playing the game of life on the winning team. That is why we not only sing the doxology or use it liturgically in worship; we live it, "for thine is the kingdom—"

Knowing that all things are in God's hands empowers us to live a focused, prayer-full life by faith. We know God is going to win this cosmic struggle and battle. We are fully planted in the present but we have faith in the future! I heard one of my mentors and "play Moms," Mrs. Marilyn Magee Talbert, say many years ago, "Our present situation is not our final destination!" That has become a part of my life and ministry. That is the hope we offer this world. That is the doxology we live by—this is God's world, God's kingdom, and God will bring it fully to pass. Eugene Peterson in *The Message* Bible translates the doxology like this: "You're in charge! You can do anything you want! You're ablaze in beauty! Yes. Yes. Yes."

The doxology helps us keep our focus in life and ministry because it reminds us that full redemption and total liberation is on the way; it will come some day! No matter how bleak it looks, how hopeless it seems, how chaotic the world, or how ragged the system, a focused, prayer-full life reminds us "we shall overcome some day." This view causes us to march to the beat of a different drummer and to dance through life to the divine melodies from heaven.

LIVING ON GOD'S SIDE

Staying focused becomes a little easier as we realize there is nothing we can do or not do, say or not say, that will hinder God's purposes from coming to pass. It shall be done! It is simply a decision of whose side do we want to find ourselves on when all is said and done. So often we hear persons say, "God is on our side!" That is the wrong view, and when we speak in those terms we have lost our focus. It is not about God being on our side but it is all about us being on God's side! God is on the side of justice, truth, righteousness, good, equality, liberation, peace, healing, love, and forgiveness; and I want to be on God's side. We live the doxology as we operate on God's side. The Lord's Prayer helps us view life and ministry from God's side and God's view. When we are on God's side—we are on the right side.

Dr. King lived in the shadow of this doxology. It can be felt as he preaches his last words before his assassination. He says:

> We've got some difficult days ahead. But it doesn't matter with me now. Because I've been to the mountaintop.... And I've looked over. And I've seen the promised land. I may not get there with you. But I want you to know tonight, that we ... will get to the promised land.... And I'm not worried about anything. I'm not fearing any [one]. Mine eyes have seen the glory of the coming of the Lord. [3]

These are the words of a focused, prayer-filled life living the doxology. It is placing all of our efforts and all of life in the hands of God, who has it all under control.

The disciples, on our behalf, asked Jesus to teach them to pray. Rather than teach them the mechanics of prayer, Jesus instead taught them and us the mechanics of how to live. Through the Lord's Prayer he gives us the model of F.O.C.U.S.-prayer-filled life, engaged in the work of the kingdom. It is not dependent upon us to accomplish, but God works through us to bring it to pass. In Christ, the kingdom has already dawned but it is through us that the kingdom becomes more visible to a world desperately needing to see it.

Therefore, we have F.O.C.U.S.-living—a life of prayer because we are people of hope. It all begins with God and ends with God. God's ultimate end and goal is the redemption and liberation of creation and humanity. We know it will be done and we not only sing the doxology but we live it through word and action. This is the lesson of what we call the model prayer, or the Lord's Prayer. Pray like it all depends on God, but live like it depends on us! This is the focused life. This is the prayer-full life. It is upon this we must build our lives, hopes, ministries, and churches. As the early church in the Book of Acts, we will turn the world upside down and then right side up, with the help of God.

The doxology solidifies and brings every area of the Lord's Prayer into focus. It is not about us; it is all about God! The kingdom's coming will not be hindered or hastened by us, but will come in God's time! The Lord's Prayer then becomes our guide and rule for living as the world gets, no matter how dimly, a glimpse of the kingdom! Lord, teach us to pray so our faith will inform us as the vision of Revelation 11:15 tells us: "The kingdom of the world has become the kingdom of our Lord / and of his [Christ], and he will reign forever and ever."

Lord, teach us to pray so the doxology will encourage us to place all of life in your hands. It will be accomplished, not in our time but in God's time. The words of the Apostle Paul in Philippians 1:6 have been a source of inspiration throughout my entire ministry, "I am confident of this, that the one who began a good work among you will bring it to completion by the day of Jesus Christ." Our lives, ministries, churches, and work are done with hope and faith because the doxology of the Lord's Prayer calls us to live with the words, "For thine is the kingdom, and the power, and the glory, for ever." Our lives, ministries, and churches will be great. Amen! It is so! It is done on earth as it is in heaven! "Lord, [now] teach us to pray…" Now, let the church say, *"Amen!"*

QUESTIONS FOR REFLECTION

1. What will you take away from this book? How is God calling you to F.O.C.U.S.?

2. Where do you need to be on God's side?

3. From your point of view, tell about a person who shows God's glory in his or her daily life.

4. If you lived the Lord's Prayer as Jesus taught, how would the church be different? How would your life be different? How would the world be different?

Appendix

St. Luke "Community" United Methodist Church

Our Mission

We are a community of God's caring people, where the gospel of Jesus Christ is proclaimed; disciples are made; and lives are transformed, equipped and empowered by the Holy Spirit to bring liberation throughout the community and world.

Our Vision

We believe God is calling us through the Holy Spirit, to a ministry of excellence, that seeks to reach all persons by providing a warm and loving Christian atmosphere, where children, youth, adults and families are nurtured and equipped to reach their God-given potential; to be an advocate for community empowerment; and a prophetic voice for all oppressed peoples with love, grace and justice as our guiding force.

OUR CORE VALUES

We "Celebrate"

Our African American Heritage & Culture

Dynamic, transformational, spirit-filled Praise &
Worship

We "Embrace"

Diversity & Inclusiveness

The caring and nurturing of "The Village"

We "Educate" through

Reflective study of the Scriptures

Supporting Academic Excellence & Higher Education

We "Dedicate" ourselves to

Community Involvement

The Struggle for Liberation & Social Justice

A lifestyle of Stewardship, Prayer and Spiritual
Discipline

Making Disciples for Jesus Christ;

and through

A Ministry of Excellence

✳✳

OUR CHURCH MOTTO

"A church reaching up to God and out into the
Community!"

NOTES

1. F.O.C.U.S.—LIVING A LIFE OF PRAYER

1. Richard Blanchard, "Fill My Cup, Lord," *African American Heritage Hymnal* (Chicago: GIA Publications, 2001), 447.

3. F.O.C.U.S.—OPEN TO THE OPPORTUNITIES

1. Desmond Tutu, *God Has a Dream: A Vision of Hope for Our Time* (New York: Doubleday Books, 2004), 15.

4. F.O.C.U.S.—CENTERED ON COMMITMENT TO FAITH

1. Civilla D. Martin, "His Eye Is on the Sparrow," *Songs of Zion* (Nashville: Abingdon, 1981).

5. F.O.C.U.S.—UNITED IN THE POWER AND MINISTRY OF RECONCILIATION

1. Annie Johnson Flint, "He Giveth More Grace," *New National Baptist Hymnal, 21st-Century Edition* (Nashville: Lillenas Publishing Company, 2001).
2. Martin Luther King, Jr., *Strength to Love* (Philadelphia: Fortress Press, 1963), 48.
3. Howard Thurman, *Jesus and the Disinherited* (Richmond, Ind.: Friends United Press, 1996), 92.
4. Martin Luther King, Jr., *Strength to Love*, 48.
5. Ibid.
6. Ibid., 49.

6. F.O.C.U.S.—STRONG AND SOLID IN THE STRUGGLE

1. Martin Luther King, Jr., *I Have a Dream: Writings and Speeches That Changed the World*, ed. James M. Washington (San Francisco: Harper San Francisco, 1986), 116.
2. Johnson Oatman, Jr., "No, Not One!" *Songs of Zion* (Abingdon Press: Nashville, 1981).
3. Frank A. Thomas, *9.11.01: African American Leaders Respond to an American Tragedy*, eds. Martha Simmons and Frank A. Thomas (Valley Forge: Judson Press, 2001), 172.
4. Horatio Richmond Palmer, "Yield Not to Temptation," *Songs of Zion* (Abingdon Press: Nashville, 1981), 62.

7. LIVING THE DOXOLOGY

1. Douglas R. A. Hare, *Interpretation: A Bible Commentary for Teaching and Preaching—The Gospel of Matthew*, ed. Paul J. Achtemeier (Louisville: John Knox Press, 1993), 67.

2. Olin P. Moyd, *Redemption in Black Theology* (Judson Press: Valley Forge, 1979), 213.

3. Martin Luther King, Jr., *I Have a Dream: Writings and Speeches That Changed the World*, ed. James M. Washington (San Francisco: HarperSanFrancisco, 1986), 203.